'Race', Class and
from School

Studies in Inclusive Education Series
Series Editor: Roger Slee
Dean of the Graduate School of Education, University of Western Australia

'Race', Class and Gender in Exclusion from School

Cecile Wright, Debbie Weekes and
Alex McGlaughlin

London and New York

First published 2000
by Falmer Press
11 New Fetter Lane, London EC4P 4EE

Simultaneously published in the USA and Canada
by Falmer Press
29 West 35th Street, New York, NY 10001

Falmer Press is an imprint of the Taylor & Francis Group

© 2000 Cecile Wright, Debbie Weekes and Alex McGlaughlin

Typeset in Times by MHL Typesetting Ltd, Coventry
Printed and bound in Great Britain by
Clays Ltd, St Ives Plc

British Library Cataloguing in Publication Data
A catalogue record for this book is available from the British Library

Library of Congress Cataloging in Publication Data
Wright, Cecile.
    'Race', class, and gender in exclusion from school/Cecile
Wright, Debbie Weekes and Alex McGlaughlin.
        p.   cm. – (Studies in inclusive education series)
    Includes bibliographical references (p.   ) and index.
    1. Discrimination in education – Great Britain Case studies.
    2. Educational equalization – Great Britain Case studies.
    I. Weekes, Debbie.   II. McGlaughlin, Alex.   III. Title.   IV. Series.
    LS212.3.G7W75   2000   99-36831
    306.43–dc21   CIP

ISBN 0-750-70842-5 (hbk)
ISBN 0-750-70841-7 (pbk)

Contents

Contents

Series Editor's Preface

'Race', Class and Gender in Exclusion from School explores the context, processes and impacts, educational and social, of exclusion from school. The recurrent identification of the causal link between school exclusion, educational failure and social exclusion establishes this book as a timely and an important addition to this series. The authors present the growing body of evidence of the racialization of school exclusion in the UK. This serves as a stark backdrop to their own research which further probes the differential experiences of pupils and excludees from a variety of ethnic groups and considers the complex matrix of relationships between race, gender and class and the deep structure of social and educational exclusion. Wright, Weekes and McGlaughlin's analysis is based upon data drawn from teachers, pupils and parents from five schools in England. The data is rich and is carefully dissected to suggest shortcomings in previous analyses of race and gender in relation to pupil exclusion.

The political context of exclusion from school in England and Wales is writ large. The authors describe Thatcher's education reforms and their sequels that etched the culture of managerialism into the educational psyche and reorganized schooling in the image of the Hayekian marketplace. Such a reform agenda provided systemic incentives for exclusion or as they so aptly put it, the 'deselection' of pupils. Market choice, the authors argue, is as much about schools choosing which pupils they do not want as it is about schools choosing which pupils they do want. Furthermore, the mantra of choice and diversity is illusory as schools are forced to narrow their teaching programmes to the narrowly defined academic requirements of the National Curriculum and thereby become less diverse as they submit to the inspectorial checklists. Add to this the reinforcement of class and racial disadvantage through the material restraints upon exercising choice and you have a policy script that inscribes disengagement, alienation and exclusion.

Drawing from their data, a case is made to support the findings of school effectiveness research that demonstrates the differences that individual schools make to pupil academic and social outcomes. The ethos created in each of the five schools has differential impacts upon exclusion, and inclusion. A number of important points are made through the presentation of the school profiles and their attitudes to pupil behaviour and their disciplinary regimes. Schools forge the inevitability of exclusion by forfeiting their own capacity to exercise judiciousness. As a Deputy Head in the cohort declares, 'We have a list of guidelines so it is largely taken out of our hands.' The particularity of the circumstances of pupil behaviour is eschewed. Schools are unlikely to acknowledge their own culpability in the behaviour of students. This latter point is vividly presented through the voices of students and parents deep into this text.

Above all, those advocating and working towards inclusive school cultures will find the extracts from student, parent and teacher interviews engaging and instructive. We learn of the dangers of essentializing race and gender in theorizing and responding to Black male exclusions. Stereotypes occlude individual student identities. This text invites us to consider other ethnic identities, a range of masculine identities and the pervasiveness of racism in the discourse of schools and teachers. The empirical data allows the reader to shift across the disparate vantage points of students, teachers and parents to unfold the layers of complexity in the structure of racism in schools which ineluctably presses students towards the margins of school life.

Black students' and communities' valuing of education while recognizing the flaws of the school experience is poignantly reconstructed through vignettes depicting teachers' lowered expectations of Black male students and the consequent disengagement of students from learning. The book offers us a serious engagement with the notion of educational right and its forfeiture through the culture-blind practices of our schools. Students' aggressive reactions to racist taunts are disconnected from the serious problem of racism. The message for students is abundantly clear; schools condone racial vilification. *'Race', Class and Gender in Exclusion from School* is an important guide to the ongoing development of more inclusive school cultures. There is much in the following pages that will be of direct benefit to educators in reflecting upon their schools and the differential experiences of their students. Such a consideration of educational cultures is an important step in furthering the project of anti-racist schooling.

Roger Slee

Acknowledgements

We would like to thank all those who contributed to the research on which this book is based.

We wish to express gratitude to the teachers, headteachers, pupils and parents who gave their time wholeheartedly and constructively. We also wish to thank Sonia Thompson for her contribution to Chapter 6 of this book and to thank Clive Pickup who assisted with the reading and offered some valuable advice, and to those not mentioned here, but who have contributed to the study.

1 Theoretical Overview

Background

The late 1990s have witnessed much debate in education on issues surrounding school achievement, discipline, disaffection and exclusion. In particular, a number of studies by local education authorities, teaching associations and the government, have drawn attention to escalating levels of exclusions from British schools (Nottinghamshire County Council 1989; SHA 1992; NUT 1992; OFSTED 1993, 1996; DfE 1992, 1994b; Parsons et al. 1997; Social Exclusion Unit 1998). This has brought educational issues to the front of the political and public arena.

The decision to exclude a child from school is the sole responsibility of the headteacher. Parents have the right to appeal against an exclusion decision. The right of headteachers to exclude a pupil from school is enshrined in the 1944 Education Act, which describes the procedure and power to exclude. Since then legislation relating to the exclusion in England and Wales has undergone several changes, most recently in the Education Act 1997 and the School Standards and Framework Act 1998. Respective change in the law has replaced the more familiar terms 'suspension' and 'expulsion' with that of 'exclusion'. The Education (No. 2) Act 1986 made provision for three types of exclusion: fixed-term, indefinite and permanent. This changed with the introduction of the Education Act 1993, which abolished the category of indefinite exclusion and limited fixed-term exclusion to 15 days in one term. The Standards and Framework Act 1998 has recently added further refinements, which include extending the period of fixed-term exclusion from 15 days in any one term to 45 days across the school year. However, the existence of exclusion as a sanction is not called into question by respective legislative changes. Thus, exclusion from school is firmly enshrined in law. It is argued that alongside official exclusions, there is of course unofficial exclusion (e.g. which is intended to be more extensive than official) (Stirling 1992). Unofficial exclusions are the 'arrangements' or 'agreements' with a parent/carer, a 'cooling off' period, or sometimes where a pupil agrees to leave a school altogether.

1

Additionally, academic and policy research has revealed that some specific groups of children and young people are more likely to experience school exclusion than are others. These vulnerable groups are more often male and with a significant proportion being African-Caribbean (CRE 1985; DfE 1992; Bourne et al. 1994; Blyth and Milner 1996). Some attempts to explain the increase in school exclusions have explored links between exclusion and a climate of increased competitiveness within schools that has resulted from a change in educational policy. One suggestion is that the continuing pressure on the educational unit of resource has increased teachers' use of time-management, with the result that teachers are less available to interact with pupils. This may very well have particular disadvantages for those pupils who are perceived as unable to contribute adequately to the overall image of the school (Blyth and Milner 1993; Bridges 1994; Hayden 1995, 1997). Pupils perceived in this way too often come from particular socio-economic and racial backgrounds (Cohen et al. 1994). Other theories have led to an examination of the cultural groupings of young males in schools, since it is known that a higher proportion of boys, especially African-Caribbean boys, experience school exclusion (Sewell 1995, 1997; Mac an Ghaill 1994).

More recent research has pointed to the financial costs of excluding children, rather than maintaining them within schools (Parsons 1996; CRE 1996). It has also been suggested that both the rights of children to education (as exemplified in Article 3 of the UN Convention on the Rights of the Child) and parental rights to choose schools for their children (as outlined in the Education Reform Act 1988) are negated when a young person experiences exclusion. It would appear that this loss of rights is further problematized by the family's racial background (Weekes and Wright 1996).

Much of the debate which has arisen out of this research, together with the increasing media attention that it has attracted, has served to heighten interest in most aspects of the exclusion issue. This interest extends from policy to pupil perspectives and includes the overall detrimental effects of exclusion on individual pupils, their parents, families and local communities. This book will both build upon and broaden existing research, by looking at how changing policies impact upon school processes, pupils, parents *and* teachers within the area of discipline and school exclusion. In doing so the book will provide much needed links between theory, which explores the impact of educational change, practice at the level of classroom delivery, and the interactions which take place between schools, teachers and their pupils. We aim to engage debate on how both educational and societal *inclusion* can be achieved, by drawing upon a thorough exploration of how policy and school exclusion affect not only the lives of excludees, but also those of their parents and teachers and the whole process of schooling.

Given that research has highlighted differential rates of exclusion among pupils, there is clearly a need for an analysis of schooling and exclusion which can explore how and why some groups of children, and some types of school, are likely to experience higher rates of exclusion than are others. This book will attempt to disentangle the factors of 'race', gender and class which impact upon the interactions between different social groups and educational institutions. Past research has explored the effects of exclusion on Black and White children and their families (Cohen et al. 1994), and pointed to the complex and often conflictual gendered relationships between White teachers and Black male pupils (Wright 1985, 1992; Sewell 1997; Mac an Ghaill 1988; Gillborn 1990; Blyth and Milner 1996). But as yet there is a lack of research which addresses *both* the school processes leading up to the exclusion of African-Caribbean, Asian and White children *and* the after effects immediately following (Gillborn and Gipps 1996).

This book will provide a much needed focus on the differential experiences of pupils by drawing upon a research project which has explored the various disciplinary processes of sanction and reward used within five very different secondary schools. The effects of these processes on pupils from a variety of racial and gendered backgrounds have also been examined. Through this approach it will be possible to highlight and explain how school processes may contribute to the over- and under-representation of different types of pupil in school exclusion statistics. Additionally, based on a series of in-depth interviews conducted with excludees, their parents, community and social workers, the book will build upon a suggestion that the effects of school exclusion extend well beyond the sphere of schooling (Blyth and Milner 1994), to include aspirations, unemployment and vulnerability to criminal behaviour. Thus the book will explore how school exclusion both leads to and exacerbates a variety of forms of *social* exclusion. One additional outcome of looking at the relationship between school and pupil is, of course, to provide data that bears upon the issue of the right to education.

In focusing on the differential race- and gender-specific experiences of pupils in schools, the book will build upon recent exclusions research work which has begun to explore pupil experiences (e.g. Garner 1994; Blyth and Milner 1996). But the book will also move beyond the majority of such work in that it will make the contribution of 'race' far more explicit; something which for the most part has been surprisingly neglected. Given that the emerging statistics show a highly disproportionate number of excluded Black pupils, the focus on 'race' within the book is especially timely. More importantly, the book will integrate this focus on 'race' with that of gender, since research has repeatedly documented the overall increase in school exclusions and under-achievement of male pupils as compared to females. Building on the most recent available work on masculinity (Mac an Ghaill 1994; Sewell 1997) the book will explore how the racial *and* gendered backgrounds of pupils impact upon their experiences of schooling.

Finally, the relationship between school exclusion and the opinions of teachers has not yet been adequately documented (de Pear and Garner 1996). This book will contribute to that documentation through an exploration of how the current climate within education, which emphasizes the improvement of standards in schools, affects both teachers' own views of their practice and their subsequent relationships with the various pupils that they teach. This will provide an important departure from earlier work on 'race' and schooling, by suggesting that the experiences of pupils in school are not merely a result of simplistic conflictual relationships between pupil and teacher, but that such interactions must be set within the wider ability of policy to dictate how 'race', gender and class are constructed and experienced within schools.

Overall the book will provide an original understanding of how the current value placed upon school exclusion within policy and society generally, is either incorporated, or countered by schools, and show how this is reflected in the extent to which they seek to exclude or include. Thus, in summary, the book will

- explore the differential experiences of pupils and excludees from a variety of ethnic groups, thereby introducing into the area of exclusions a much-needed focus on 'race';
- look at the *wider* processes involved in exclusion, as well as the after-effects of exclusion;
- provide important and necessary links between policy and practice.

As we have noted, the increasing evidence of pupils being temporarily and permanently excluded from school is a matter of concern for the public, professionals and government alike (e.g. Social Exclusion Unit 1998). Notwithstanding the argument that the issue of exclusion is complex and the problem extensive, what becomes evident is the overlapping of the development of education policies since the 1980s and the increasing rates of school exclusions. There is no doubt that these elements are closely connected. Thus, it will be argued that each is both the cause and the consequence of the other.

Educational Policy

Black minorities have frequently been casualties of rules and procedures which may not have been intended to discriminate against them but which, in effect, do so and there is considerable resistance when hitherto taken-for-granted procedures are brought into question.

(Rattansi 1992: 23)

It has been argued widely that the increase in exclusions is directly related to changes in the organization of the education system which began in the late 1980s. Much of the literature that exists within the area of exclusions has focused on links between this and the creation of a 'free market' in education, following the 1988 Education Reform Act (ERA) (Bourne, Bridges and Searle 1994; Stirling 1992; Cohen et al. 1994). This literature suggests that many of the basic principles set out in the 1998 ERA, especially those which relate to academic performance (the publication of examination results in school league tables), and parental choice (the movement in schools towards open enrolment), have created a climate which emphasizes competitiveness and individualism (Bash 1989; McVicar 1990). It is within this ethos that some parents and children will be more able to compete than others (Blyth and Milner 1993; Stirling 1992). The 1988 Act proposed far-reaching changes to British education, which had differing effects on the nature of school exclusions. The main proposal was the introduction of a national curriculum, together with a method of assessing its effectiveness, with the intention of improving the position of British children in relation to their European counterparts. The Act also sought to reduce LEA control of schools by allowing local authority maintained schools to 'opt out', transferring responsibility for budgetary decisions to individual schools. Additionally, it extended the notion of 'parental choice' in selection of schools, originally set out in the 1981 Education Act, through advancing the concept of 'open enrolment'. This, in effect, removed the ability of LEAs to set limits on the number of children allowed into each school, whilst allowing parents to seek places for their children beyond the boundaries of catchment area and even local authority (Bridges 1994). It has also been surmised by some researchers and commentators within the field of education, that the concepts of 'parental choice' and 'opting out' contribute to the creation of an education system which is racially segregated, since they enable some White parents to avoid schools with what they perceive as too many Black pupils (Bridges 1994; Macey 1992; Troyna 1990).

Though it may be difficult to establish the direct effects of educational policy from the late 1980s on the exclusion of children from secondary schools, it is possible to outline the various impacts of the 'market system' of education on the ways in which different groups of pupils are responded to in schools.

Using Hayden's (1995) comments on the 'quasi market' system existing within current education policy, it is possible to identify the processes by which pupils are constructed as 'marketable' or otherwise and which could have an effect upon their educational careers. The 'market' philosophy within education is based upon a need to improve efficiency, cost consciousness and adequate utilization of resources. However, parents are placed differentially within this consumerist context. Thus, social divisions of race and class impact upon parents' choice of school, and vice versa (Young and Halsey 1995). This then impacts upon the general marketability of children from different class and racial backgrounds. This fact becomes highly relevant when it is considered that children from ethnic minority and working-class backgrounds feature disproportionately in exclusions figures. Within this context, exclusion has been implemented as a form of regulation and selection where 'the difficult pupil must either be seen as an object of punishment or a drain on resources' (Cohen et al. 1994: 2).

The changed financial arrangements resulting from Local Management of Schools (LMS) and brought about by the 1988 Act, has meant that each school now has the responsibility of buying in professional services for children experiencing emotional and behavioural difficulties. In view of cost, and the market ethos of efficiency, the provision of these extra services may no longer be regarded as a priority within many schools and in any case is limited. Thus, the needs of such children will not be met despite research which has shown that the problems of children with learning and/or emotional difficulties often manifest themselves in disruptive behaviour (Hayden 1995).

Because of reduced resources in schools for the support of children with behavioural difficulties, and the implementation of the national curriculum, teachers have less time to spend with individual children exhibiting these or other problems within the classroom (Blyth and Milner 1993; Stirling 1992; NUT 1992). The national curriculum has also added to already high levels of stress among teachers, as it limits flexibility and autonomy within teaching and increases the accountability of schools through the measurement of performance (Blyth and Milner 1993). This can be seen to have affected the overall teacher/pupil relationship which again does not create a climate sympathetic to the needs of children.

The concept of 'choice' which educational policy created for parents, became particularly problematic for some groups of parents and children. Choice not only connected with the marketability of the child, but also had racialized implications, e.g. the over-representation of Black children in exclusion statistics. The existence of racialized stereotypes, relating to the confrontational nature of relationships between Black male pupils and White teachers is well documented (Gillborn 1990; Wright 1985; Mac an Ghaill 1988; Sewell 1997). Thus, notions of 'choice' raised issues in relation to the 'choices' offered to Black parents of children who have been or are at risk of being excluded (Bourne, Bridges and Searle 1994; Cohen et al. 1994).

The most recent education legislation is the Standards and Framework Act 1998. At the heart of this reform is the commitment to raising education standards, reducing school exclusions and increasing the involvement of parents in children's education. There is a modification of the open enrolment policy and the grant maintained schools and city technology provision. However, the marketization of schooling clearly remains, with the retention of local management of schools and the annual publication of performance tables based on national assessment tests (otherwise known as 'league tables').

The Act comments on the experiences of ethnic minority children within the British education system, specifically to do with their relatively poor academic performance and their disproportionate representation within the exclusion statistics. Despite this, there are no strategies provided for addressing these areas. Thus, one commentator has suggested that the conclusion to be drawn from the recent reform is that ' "initiatives" relating to effective schools, improving schools, value-adding schools, and all the rest of them, are for the next five years at least to be colour-blind, culture-blind, racism-blind' (Richardson 1998: 23).

A recent report by the Social Exclusion Unit (1998) has set national targets for the reduction of exclusions: 'that by 2002 there will be a one-third reduction in the number of both permanent and fixed-term exclusions'. Yet, despite the report's acknowledgement of the disproportionate exclusion of pupils from ethnic minorities, there is no race dimension to the target set for reducing exclusions. In other words, the first ever national target for reducing exclusions is 'colour-blind'.

> By failing to stipulate a specific target for a reduction in the exclusion of Black children the way is left clear for the situation to persist or even worsen. Previous research suggests that Black children are unlikely to share equally in any improvement, and that by 2002, therefore, we would be in a position where the relative over-representation of Black children has actually grown.
>
> (Majors, Gillborn and Sewell 1998)

The Significance of 'Race', Gender, Class and Culture in Exclusion from School

The section above examined the ways in which education policies have provided a context within which school exclusions have taken place. The aim of this section is to identify how policy interrelates with experience within the classroom to produce increasing rates of exclusion. In doing so it explores gender, ethnicity and cultural factors within exclusion from school.

As mentioned earlier, statistics reveal that some groups of children and young people are at considerably greater risk of exclusion than others. The research evidence indicates that those who are at disproportionate risk of exclusion are African-Caribbean boys of both primary and secondary school age (e.g. Hayden 1997; Parsons 1996; Wright 1992; Gillborn and Gipps 1996). However, the picture is clouded because some LEAs do not record the ethnic background of excluded pupils (Cohen et al. 1994; CRE 1985; DfE 1992; Mayet 1992; Nottinghamshire County Council 1989). The over-representation of Black pupils in the numbers excluded from mainstream schooling is not new (e.g. Coard 1971; Tattum 1982; CRE 1985). The latest DfE statistics show that boys account for an overwhelming majority of all exclusions (83 per cent of permanent exclusions in 1995–96). But within this total OFSTED and the DfE have shown that African-Caribbean boys are 4–5 times more likely to be excluded than their White peers. More recently, exclusion statistics indicate that in some areas African-Caribbean boys were up to 15 times more likely to be excluded from school than are their White classmates (TES, 1998b). Disruptive and aggressive behaviour are the most prominent among the reasons given for the exclusion of these pupils.

More generally, any focus on African-Caribbean pupils in the exclusion process has meant that other minority groups' experiences of the process has been reflected in the published research to date. Asian pupils have been traditionally under-represented in the school exclusion statistics. Recent statistics, however, are suggesting that exclusions of Asian pupils are on the increase in some local authorities, particularly among Pakistani boys (TES 1998b). A recent study in Birmingham for the academic years 1994/95 and 1995/96, confirmed that African-Caribbean boys are disproportionately over-represented in the permanent exclusion statistics but also shows an increase in the permanent exclusion of Asian pupils from secondary school, particularly Pakistani boys (Mehra 1998). This supports the findings of an earlier OFSTED Survey which revealed that: 'An increasing number of LEAs are aware of, and concerned about, the disproportionate numbers of majority ethnic pupils, in particular boys of Caribbean and African heritage (but increasingly also boys of Pakistani heritage) being excluded (OFSTED 1996: 27).

The most striking aspect of this trend in exclusions is the apparent interrelationship between gender, ethnicity, culture and social disadvantage. Central to an understanding of the reason why certain ethnic minority groups feature disproportionately in exclusion statistics is an examination of the school processes which lead to exclusion.

There is a growing body of research evidence which suggests that the exclusion of Black pupils reflects on the one hand, the nature of teacher–pupil relationships – characterized by complex, differential expectations and assumptions, and on the other hand, Black pupils' response to their experience of schooling. Researchers (e.g. Mac an Ghaill 1988; Gillborn 1990; Wright 1987, 1992; Sewell 1997) have studied the processes which lead to the ultimate sanction of exclusion and all have concluded that relations between White teachers and Black pupils is characterized by conflict. Wright, for instance, suggests that despite intentions and commitments to equality, White teachers on the whole perceive and respond to African-Caribbean students in ways which are detrimental towards them. They are likely to be singled out for criticism when practising the same behaviour as their White peers. In support of this observation, their contemporaries of all other ethnic groups, judged the treatment meted out to African-Caribbean pupils to be both unequal and unfairly harsh (Sewell 1997; Mirza 1992; Gillborn 1990). By way of explanation Wright (1987) points to the underlying expectations and assumptions held by White teachers about their Black pupils, not least a belief that African-Caribbean culture is characterized by a general rejection of authority. Sanction rationales were based on the need to immediately 'nip in the bud' and respond harshly to any problem which might occur. This unequal practice became the source of much conflict between pupil and teacher. Those African-Caribbean pupils who contested or resisted the teachers' unequal treatment were deemed to be displaying authority-rejection behaviour and viewed as problematic. Wright (1987) also found that whereas teachers had a tendency to conflate education and schooling when weighing up the pupils, the pupils themselves did not do so.

The concept of 'resistance' in relation to schooling has been employed by a number of writers keen to explore how specific groups of pupils negotiate and respond to their marginal positions in schools, whilst avoiding a determinist analysis of the ability of schools to reproduce these social and cultural inequalities. The work of Paul Willis (1977) attempted to interrogate the division between structure and agency that earlier social reproduction accounts had introduced. However, Willis's work has been criticized as dualistic and determinist (Walker 1986).

Further studies on the topic of resistance have noted that pupil responses to the schooling process can be interpreted in ways different from those of Willis (1977). Working class pupils are not the only ones found to resist schooling (Aggleton 1987; Watson 1993). Class may not always be implicated in pupil resistance (Meyenn 1980). The notion of specific pupil groups being consistently anti-school in their attitudes has been shown to be simplistic as researches have shown, for example, that African-Caribbean male pupils demonstrate attitudes that are both pro-school and anti-school (Gillborn 1990; Sewell 1997). Such findings are a counterpoint to that research which focuses on the disaffection of African-Caribbean pupils (Harrel 1995; Mac an Ghaill 1988; Cashmore and Troyna 1982). Research has also shown that it is the perception of teacher authoritarian roles that are rejected and not education as such (Sewell 1997). Earlier research revealed that it is the racialized and gendered discrimination which pupils perceive in their teachers that is rejected and not the importance of education (Fuller 1982).

Pupils bring into schools their racialized and gendered positions and these interact with their dispositions towards power. Bourdieu (1977) has suggested that pupils have a constantly reformulated set of dispositions towards power, primarily rooted in social class. Race and class are inextricably intertwined in questions of how pupils are disposed to the power relations they experience in schooling. How 'race' defines the educational experience is clearly connected to class background and is also defined in opposition to the predominantly White middle-class background of education professionals.

Having said this, race alone may influence the experiences of pupils in school. Research by Horvat (1997) has shown that race in itself is a powerful influence in shaping school experiences. Thus:

> Often, this racial influence functions most effectively as a marker of class membership and position.
>
> (Horvat 1997: 13)

Other studies also argue for the interrelation of race and gender in the exploration of black experience (e.g. Mama 1995).

The complex ways in which gender and race intersect in the experiences of Black pupils does require more examination. The gendered differences between Black pupils has indeed been used to explain the differing adaptations of pupils and rates of academic achievement (e.g. Woods 1990; Mirza 1992; Gillborn and Gipps 1996).

As will be shown in the accounts of the young people interviewed in the present study, and presented particularly in Chapters 3, 4 and 5, resistance was often located in pupils' wider racialized and gendered positions. Forms of speech, dress and ways of walking are often indicative of displaced contestations or resistances (Aggleton 1987) and these expressions hold greater cultural currency when used in an area (school) where Black pupils are in a numerical and power-related minority.

Deracialized Policy – Racializing Exclusions

This chapter set out to provide an overview of the context in which the rise in school exclusions witnessed in the 1990s has taken place. It has attempted to locate the increase in exclusions within wider issues of educational policy, particularly the marketization of schooling. Although education policy over the last 15 years has de-emphasized racialized positions as a significant factor in the education process (Gillborn 1997), within the context of school, exclusion and sanction has become increasingly racialized as exemplified by the disproportionate frequency of exclusions of African-Caribbean pupils (TES 1998a). Policy has exacerbated the problem of exclusion: there has been a reinforcement of the concept of the 'ideal' pupil by emphasizing cost efficiency, examination performance and marketization in schools. Therefore, disruptive pupils are seen as costly in financial terms and in terms of league table performance. In this context and climate schools may be less likely to see their role as being inclusive, i.e. education for all. They may see some pupil groups as a liability. Hence, the current educational climate, with its emphasis on raising standards and improving discipline, will continue to extend the powers of schools to apply greater sanctions to pupils.

Methodology

The study on which this book is based was an attempt to explore the school processes which led to the exclusion of Black children from secondary school. Research was conducted over two years in a large education authority which has a small but growing minority ethnic population. Many years prior to this study, work was conducted within the education authority which showed alarming disparities between the exclusion of Black children compared to their White counterparts.

The aims of this study were to explore and document the nature and pattern of secondary school exclusions of pupils from ethnic groups in general and to identify the school processes which may lead to the exclusion of African-Caribbean pupils in particular. In view of the disproportionate level of exclusions of such pupils from school, both nationally and locally, the study is also concerned with exploring the nature of educational provision for African-Caribbean male pupils permanently excluded from mainstream schooling. In brief, the study involved surveying all secondary schools in one county education authority, in order to assess the overall pattern of exclusions; extensive interviews with pupils and staff in five representative secondary schools; and additional interviews with a small group of African-Caribbean male pupils who had experienced permanent exclusion from school.

The bulk of the research was conducted within the five selected schools, which varied according to their local authority status, the characteristics of the local catchment area and the nature of their pupil intake. Three of the schools were under local authority control, whilst of the other two, one was a technology college and the other enjoyed grant maintained community school status. The schools were primarily selected according to the proportion of their pupils who were from ethnic backgrounds. Represented among the five selected for study were schools with low, average or higher than average proportions of African and African-Caribbean pupils. By this means it was possible to explore the relationship between the numbers of Black children attending and the school processes which led to the exclusion of Black children. A total of 62 pupils and 52 members of teaching staff were interviewed from the five schools in the research sample. Twenty-five of these pupils were of African-Caribbean/mixed parentage. The pupils interviewed were from Years 9 and 10 only (age range 13–15 years). As far as possible, nine pupils from each year group and an even mix of African-Caribbean, Asian and White pupils were selected for interview. The pupils were recruited for interview by Heads of Year, with each pupil selected either having previously been excluded from school, or having experienced a number of school sanctions (i.e. being withdrawn from lessons, referred to on-site units or placed on report). Three of the nine pupils from each year were White, three Asian and three African-Caribbean. The educational abilities of the pupils varied.

In addition to these pupils, 12 African-Caribbean young people and their parents were also interviewed. These young people had experienced permanent and fixed-period exclusions from other schools in the local authority. All but one of these young people were male, with two being of mixed parentage and the remainder African-Caribbean. One parent of each child was also interviewed, the aim of these interviews being to explore the immediate consequences of school exclusion for the parent and child. These interviewees were all recommended by a local community worker and exclusions advocate which importantly set these parents and children out as a group eager to gain adequate educational resources for their children, and also to go on to appeal decisions.

The Local Authority

The city within which all five schools researched, and the 12 interviewees described above, were situated had high rates of youth unemployment, particularly among Black men aged 18–25. Of African-Caribbean men 47.5 per cent were unemployed as were 44.5 per cent of Pakistani young men. Approximately 11 per cent of the local authority population were minority ethnic residents with 3.4 per cent of the population being African-Caribbean. African-Caribbean young people constitute approximately 3–6 per cent of the population aged between 10–15. Within the city itself where the majority of minority ethnic individuals had settled, 7.1 per cent of the total population were Black. The education authority served a wide variety of schools each serving diverse pupil groups. In certain areas, White residents constituted almost all of the local population, creating particularly charged environments either in the school or local area.

Within the city, minority ethnic pupils constitute 20.8 per cent of the school population, and Black pupils in particular, comprise 9.7 per cent. Again Black children were not distributed equally throughout all areas of the city. However, Black children, were given 11 per cent of permanent exclusions in the city and 14 per cent of fixed-period exclusions. There was an increase in the exclusion of Black children from primary schools in the city which in the previous year had stood at 15 per cent, but had now risen to 21 per cent. There were clear disproportionate exclusions of Black children within the city and throughout the five schools studied. It is within this context that statements about the disproportionate exclusions of Black pupils can be made. Such rates of exclusion for these groups have been well documented recently (Social Exclusion Unit 1998; Osler 1997). Rather it is the intention of this book to explore the specific policy-based, school-constructed, racialized, gendered and (teacher/pupil) relational processes which culminate in disproportionate figures. What precipitates the cycles of exclusion that African-Caribbean boys in particular find themselves caught up in? How can theorizing educational right provide an additional means of understanding parental responses not only to exclusion, but to the ways in which they *parent* their children to survive schooling?

These are some of the important questions that any current debate on the issue of school exclusion now needs to tackle in order to engender a new discussion around race, gender, schooling and the life chances of African-Caribbean young people.

Structure of the Book

Chapter 2 looks more closely at the nature of the empirical study on which the book is based and provides an analysis of the five schools which took part. It will attempt to look at the value placed upon either sanction or reward in each school, and link this to the ethnic composition of student and teacher populations, and the schools' social class background, (as evidenced by proportion of school meals, and parental occupation of the pupils studied). In doing so, it will begin to trace how the significance of exclusion, or inclusion, characterized the nature of relationships between school and pupil. In this chapter it will therefore be suggested that assessing the ethos of schools is important for situating the relationships which take place within them. The views of headteachers and senior managers will also prove important to exploring the concept of school *ethos*, as, though (particularly maintained) if schools are accountable to various aspects of educational policy on discipline, exclusion and provision, there will exist varied interpretations of policy among senior school staff. It will be suggested that these interpretations will also be linked to the ways in which race, class and gender are structured in schools, by virtue of their racial, gendered and class-specific pupil intakes and geographical locations. The way that other agencies are perceived by senior staff will also impinge upon the nature of this 'ethos' (e.g. Section 11 teachers, educational psychologists and community groups). Through this, the chapter will provide an assessment of the interrelationship of institutional attitudes towards discipline and the wider concepts of 'race', gender and class.

Following on from the previous chapter's introduction of differential school philosophies on discipline, Chapter 3 looks at the way these impinge upon the differential responses of pupils to school. It explores whether the concept of resistance (Aggleton 1987), is relevant to the experiences of the pupils researched. Chapter 3 also assesses how the pupils and teachers in the study responded to each other, given each school's position on school exclusion, and explores whether it is necessary to speak of these relationships in terms of power and powerlessness. It is also particularly revealing, given the nature of existing work on exclusion, and pupils in schools, to explore the relationship of teacher to institution, and look at how resistance (or contestation) manifests itself in relation to individual teacher commitment to inclusion.

Chapter 4 looks at ways that the experiences of young people in school vary in relation to their gendered and racial backgrounds. Building on feminist research on gender (Anyon 1983; Davies 1984) and the increasing area of work on schooling masculinities (Mac an Ghaill 1994; Sewell 1997), the chapter looks at the ways that masculinities and femininities are produced within the schools researched and how it is necessary to be able to explore how *both* concepts fuse with that of 'race'. This provides an important contribution to the literature, which has often looked separately at either masculinity or femininity. The chapter will also look at how different racial masculinities and femininities are produced in relation to the racial and gendered backgrounds of teachers. This will be used to provide an additional perspective on the issue of power relations explored in Chapter 3. Chapter 5 takes up many of the issues explored around masculinity to look at the necessity of including an analysis of Black girls' experiences of school sanction and teacher interaction and how teachers 'feminize' aggressive behaviour which they simultaneously perceive as masculine and 'unlady-like'. The chapter asserts the difficulties some staff face when attempting to gender misbehaviour.

Chapter 6 looks at a number of case studies that focus on the effects of exclusion upon young African-Caribbean males. It explores how African-Caribbean excludees and their parents talk about their relationships to school and wider society in view of the restrictions exclusion places upon them. It will also be possible to chart how excluded identities are created, through assessing the extent to which excludees and their parents felt that they were either subject to a school emphasis on exclusion, or other extenuating factors. Importantly it introduces into the exclusion debate issues surrounding educational rights and the lack of parental rights for those parenting Black children to cope with the stresses of school-based racism. The social consequences of exclusion, in view of employment/training choices, or vulnerability to crime, will also be highlighted through discussing how the lives of the excludees have developed over time.

The book will conclude by referring back to the discussion developed in earlier chapters. In doing this, it will look at ways in which negative social consequences, such as those highlighted in Chapter 6, can be avoided. It will outline possible recommendations, based on the experiences presented in the book, and the various forms of support that schools, teachers and parents have drawn on. The chapter examines processes of intervention in the management of pupils in schools, and explores the possibilities involved in focusing on inclusion, rather than exclusion in schools. Through initiatives such as pupil–pupil mentoring, monitoring of behaviour, increased focus on rewards and support for marginalized pupils, it will be suggested that perceptions of disaffected groups of pupils, and the pupils' perceptions of themselves, can be significantly and positively altered within educational institutions.

2   School Ethos and the 'Value' of Exclusion

Introduction

There is an increasing body of work highlighting the important difference that individual schools make to pupil achievement (Reynolds and Cuttance 1992; Mortimore et al. 1988). Schools can also make a difference to the educational *experience* of a child and research has noted that there are different rates of exclusion between individual schools (OFSTED 1996). A variety of explanations abound as to why exclusion rates vary between schools, including those relating to pupil intake, geographical area and deteriorating pupil behaviour (SHA 1992). However it has also been suggested that the views of headteachers, and the school policies which they implement contribute to these discrepancies (Benson 1996; Imich 1994; McManus 1987). Headteachers and senior management staff place a high value on the use of exclusion as a school sanction, which in turn creates a particular ethos on discipline. It will be suggested here that assessing the ethos of a school is important for situating the relationships which take place within it. The concept of school ethos, therefore, can provide an illuminating perspective on the relationship between institutional definitions of adequate discipline and wider concepts of 'race', gender and class.

Effective schools are based upon a particular school ethos which is an integration of the opinions of all staff around specific disciplinary and learning issues. Ineffective schools exhibit cultures which are unsupportive. They fail to adopt systems of support/sanctions, shared understandings and staff support, and means by which pupils can discuss issues on a regular basis. Effective home–school relationships are not developed or maintained. Instead they tend to blame the pupils and shift responsibility to outside agencies (DES Elton report 1989). Indeed exclusion may say more about the needs of the school than it does about the pupil being excluded. Imich (1994) contends that institutional factors may even predict exclusion better than the behaviour of the pupil involved.

Institutional Contexts and Differences in Rates of Exclusion

Research on school processes, most notably Rutter et al. (1979), has emphasized the importance of school effects, stressing in particular the role of school 'ethos' as a major variable in how an individual child or behaviour is viewed. Other studies in the late 1970s and during the 1980s (Reynolds et al. 1976; Galloway et al. 1982) support this claim. Some research specifically demonstrated the importance of school organization and ethos in relation to how minor matters could escalate into suspension and other offences (Galloway et al. 1982; Lawrence et al. 1984). Thus exclusion was not an inevitable consequence to a particular set of events but a product of a set of events dealt with in a certain way. Such research raises a number of important points; notably the very real processes and effects created by education policy, suggesting that some schools respond to the pressures of operating in a quasi-market, by becoming more willing to work with the successful and with those who are considered to be more amenable. Troyna (1990) argues that the ERA forced schools to become more efficient and placed them within a free market context compelling them to give less priority to individual needs, with little emphasis allotted to equality issues. Instead the tendency has been to look upon the cost-effectiveness of different pupils. This trend is more effectively resisted where Black and other minority parents constitute a significant proportion of the local community.

Morgan (1997) suggests that agencies such as schools operate as societies in microcosm, with their own cultures and sub-cultures. Other aspects of organizational culture include an institutional common history, shared meanings and beliefs about effective ways in which to get things accomplished. Much of this can be subsumed under the terms 'school ethos' and 'the hidden curriculum'. For example, individual schools display different emphases towards discipline, racism, co-operation and account-ability to parents and the local community. Interestingly, Morgan also warns organizations that their own intentions can be distorted by the emphasis that many agencies have placed on the issue of finance.

> [T]ake the way in which financial considerations may be allowed to shape the reality of an organization through the routine operation of financial information systems. Under the influence of these kinds of control, people or organizational units, whether they be pupils in schools, patients in hospital, or work teams in manufacturing plants, may be translated into profit centers generating costs and revenues. Those systems may not be seen as cultural in nature. But they definitely are, their influence may be far more pervasive than other programs that are explicitly designed to create cultural change, for example in relation to the enhancement of 'quality production' or the empowerment of staff.
>
> (Morgan 1997: 144)

The financial imperative in schools is gauged in terms of teacher effort, thus the culture of the school is influenced by the way that it envisages/responds to inter-school competition and the priority afforded efficiency and economy as measured in terms of SATs results and league-table positioning. The image which the school's staff has of itself and attempts to project into the community, effectively determines the ways in which the school is run. This is ultimately reflected in the amount of teacher effort that an organization deems acceptable to spend on the average and the exceptional pupil. Each school will have developed norms as to what is considered acceptable effort to expend on different types of pupils who have been allocated to categories such as the 'deserving' and the 'undeserving'.

The variation in rates of exclusion across schools is an issue which greatly interests professionals concerned with supporting schools and facilitating the admission of excluded pupils to new schools (Robotham 1995). Rates of exclusion reflect high bureaucratic involvement in pastoral care, discipline and the unintended consequences of some procedures in some schools. Certainly pastoral support networks are an essential element in combating exclusion. Thus schools with low exclusion rates have clear policies in operation and guidelines for ensuring that cases are dealt with in a supportive manner. Similarly there are opportunities to discuss rather than react to problems as they arise, as exemplified by an open approach with opportunities for mediation. The Education Reform Act (ERA) operates in such a way that many of the needs of children have been crowded out by the national curriculum, with pupils ranking it as the third most important contributory factor in disaffection (Kinder et al. 1996b). It has even reduced the time available for Personal Social Education, which is recognized as an effective and legitimate means for offering pastoral support (OFSTED 1996). The ERA's emphasis on high achievers has resulted in the lowest achievers being left out of the national targets for education and training. OFSTED (1996) and the DfE (1992) have identified clearly observable school effects in the patterns of exclusion, with half of secondary schools excluding one or no pupils (Donovan 1998). Indeed the overall rates of exclusion were found to vary by ten times between some local authorities (Parsons 1996), leading the DfEE (1997) to argue that school, ethnic and LEA variations were unacceptable. LEAs have a vital role to play in the reduction of school exclusion offering guidelines, policies and support to schools. Unfortunately, the introduction of league tables has led to schools shifting resources in ways which have maximized academic results rather than the needs of the disaffected (Pearce and Hillman 1998). This is not surprising, given that 'unsuccessful' schools have been punished in a range of ways which can ultimately lead to closure.

School Culture and Managerialism

Although schools have much in common with each other, as organizations they also differ in terms of the specific patterns of interaction between different groups and individuals, the language used and the approach adopted to deal with various situations. Thus understanding the ethos and culture of schools generally and the particular approach taken by specific schools to the issue of exclusion will shed light on the vulnerability of Black children to this ultimate school sanction. At its most basic, organizational culture refers to a set of core beliefs and assumptions which are held by members of an establishment. As such it underpins the ways in which the institution operates and the ways its employees, volunteers and contributors are expected to behave (Schein 1992). At the heart of any organization lies a range of discourses about the values and beliefs that underpin it, which dictate how its members are expected to behave. Organizational culture refers to those aspects which characterize the organization's approach to day-to-day functioning and more importantly how employees are expected to respond to controversy. Exclusion, and the exclusion of any one particular group (whether intentional or not) falls into this category. Organizational culture is able to highlight many of these discrepancies and suggest what effects they might have on the behaviour of those who find themselves in conflict with the dominant organizational culture. For instance, the wider social culture via law defines what constitutes a school, and who is recognized as qualified as a teacher. It is government which determines the nature of the curriculum in state and grant maintained schools. Indeed there is much which unites schools in Britain, ranging from statutory require-ments, social relations between the pupil and the teacher, to the wider social attitudes on 'race' relations. Consequently, regardless of individual school, geographical area, etc., African-Caribbean children as a group tend to share many similar educational experiences and a higher than average vulnerability to exclusion. Thus the notion of organizational culture offers a way of illuminating what may be happening within schools, as organizations, with regard to exclusion, and is a particularly useful concept given the recent economic and political pressures placed on schools to compete with each other in a pseudo-market environment. These pressures inevitably have given rise to new ways of perceiving pupils and managing the school as a learning environment. Over the past decade and a half, schools as organizations have faced tremendous challenges (e.g. curricular, inspection, financial constraints, threat of closure, competition) and in response to these pressures many have adopted managerialist techniques. Pollitt (1993: 1) describes managerialism as 'a set of beliefs and practices, at the core of which burns the seldom-tested assumption that better management will prove an effective solvent for a range of economic and social ills'.

Key to managerialism is the notion that social progress remains dependent upon rising productivity and economic measurement. It suggests that the way to a promising and more productive future lies in the new and ever more advanced technologies and the application of these ideals relies on employees who are 'disciplined in accordance with the productivity ideal'

(Alvesson 1987: 158). Given the central role of managers in planning, implementing and measuring this new productivity, they expect and are granted the right to manage (Pollitt 1993). Moreover, at an ideological level managers were envisaged as possessing a range of transferable skills. Thus any good manager would be capable of managing any organization, whether it lies in the public, the private or the voluntary sector – as exemplified by Lord Sainsbury's involvement in the management of the NHS. The political climate of the 1980s was just ripe for managerialism, and as an ideology and set of practices it flourished under the guidance and support of Thatcherism, with a particular stress on the superiority of the private over the public sector. Indeed this way of operating is sometimes linked with neo-Taylorism principally because of its capacity to be applied to the public sector. Certainly one of the major reforms in management terms has been the application of these ideas on non-manual workers, including teachers. Thus in an effort to discipline the workforce, there has been a rise in, and bureaucratization of, the structure of control and the measurement of effort or work levels. Characteristic of these changes has been the development of performance indicators, individual performance review and performance-related pay, all of which have currency in recent debates on super-teachers. Another unfortunate tendency of managerialism is its stress on those areas which are easiest to measure, i.e. economy and efficiency over and above the dimension of effectiveness, with accompanying cruder performance indicators, such as examination results, over and above those which measure retaining 'difficult' children in school. Managerialism developed within an anti-equal opportunities climate, where pro-equality agencies were being vilified in the media as being more concerned with political correctness than fairness, and creating tensions where there were none.

Public sector acceptance of managerialism in a non-critical manner fails to recognize the distinctive philosophy, purpose, conditions and task basis for the management of such agencies and the conflict between this and the nature and philosophy of schooling. Without concrete plans, tools and commitment to combat the socio-political and institutional culture of managerialism, the problems of high exclusion rates will remain, and African-Caribbean pupils will continue to experience the brunt of these procedures.

Certainly at a macro level, exclusion rates for African-Caribbeans remain relatively consistent between LEAs, with Black pupils experiencing the highest rates of any ethnic group. Clearly authorities have not devised national ethnically based exclusion policies, therefore wider social structures are operating to create similarly skewed ethnic exclusion rates at the level of the school. This has obvious implications for the state given the role that it plays in overseeing the quality and nature of educational provision. Hence perceiving schools as organizations, with cultures shaped by wider socio-economic surroundings, provides a framework within which to understand the macro-mezza and individual dimensions of Britain's skewed exclusion rates.

The shift in emphasis towards market principles has resulted in a corresponding shift in the organizational culture of many schools, such that 'need' has come to be viewed as both costly and problematic. Through the confines of managerialism diversity could also be viewed as too expensive to sustain. Diversity is a difficult but essential aspect for today's schools to manage. Facing the many challenges to the success of any school requires that it develop and maintain rituals, norms and shared ways of operating which contribute to that success. 'Successful' schools are able to build cohesive cultures, so they move beyond slogans, empty vision statements and policies to affect all levels of the agency. It requires inclusive rather than exclusive practices, and leadership style can contribute to this process. For example, a stress upon harmony and/or discipline, over and above airing and resolving conflict, may exacerbate splits between cultural groups without creating effective ways forward.

Competition between schools via the league tables and its administration through the employment of managerialist techniques, has led to the prominence of efficiency and economy measures rather than effectiveness. One example of this is the continuing emphasis on credentials for the benefit of the greatest number – which leaves those with 'different' needs fending for themselves. Effectiveness in terms of meeting particular social and personal goals or moving pupils as far towards their potential as possible are less easy matters to measure. As a group Black children are expensive and fail the managerialist test. They pull heavily on the effectiveness area and this is not helpful for schools which are being officially measured on other areas, such as economy and efficiency.

The Schools

Within the five schools which participated in the research, there were different approaches around the issue of school exclusion. These almost always reflected the viewpoints of the Headteacher and certain members of senior management, not only because the decision to exclude was the responsibility of these individuals, but also because they were responsible for creating individual school policies. All policies, including that which may have related specifically to school exclusion and discipline, were influential on the wider school ethos around exclusion/inclusion. This ethos consisted not only of Headteacher opinion on the use of sanction, but also the place of equal opportunities and rewards policies within the overall structure of the school, together with the degree of tension or support for these issues among staff and pupils.

School A

School A was situated in the middle of a fairly wealthy suburb in the city, and performed very well within the education authority in terms of GCSE

A–C grades obtained. The majority of the pupil population was drawn from the immediate area and therefore many of the pupils came from skilled, managerial and/or professional families. Minority ethnic residents comprised at least 6.15 per cent of the total population in the area which was mainly White. The proportion of White residents in the local area was greater than that throughout the city and only 1.6 per cent of the local population were African-Caribbean and African. There was an equally small minority ethnic population within the school. However, these pupils were perceived as being highly visible by many of the teachers. Black pupils constituted approximately 7 per cent of all pupils whilst Indian pupils constituted approximately 9 per cent, and Pakistani pupils, 5.6 per cent of all pupils. School A was under local authority control.

The exclusions of pupils from school in the year following the research involved a total of 52 pupils, out of a school roll of approximately 824 pupils. The rate of exclusions therefore was low here in comparison to many of the other schools studied. However 29 per cent of all exclusions were of African-Caribbean male pupils. No Black females were excluded. Two further exclusions involved Pakistani boys and one involved an Indian boy whilst the remaining exclusions were of White pupils. Clearly then, Black pupils were excluded far more often than their numbers in the school population would justify.

The emphasis on discipline within the school was average. At morning briefings pastoral managers would inform tutors and other teaching staff about returning excludees and children who were likely to be in the on-site unit. There was a high emphasis on achievement throughout the school and all senior staff interviewed felt that temporary school exclusions were necessary. Both the Head and the Deputy Head however, did not particularly like to use permanent exclusions and the rate for this was quite low. Guidelines for procedures to be taken should a pupil give staff cause for concern were made clear within staff handbooks. Assistance would be given to classroom teachers, by members of senior management, should an incident arise. However, the decision to temporarily exclude usually lay with the Deputy Head who felt that staff were often too eager to call on his assistance for what were frequently simple disciplinary issues.

School B

School B was situated near a large housing estate in the centre of the city. The surrounding area consisted again of mainly White residents – 90.7 per cent of the local population were White, compared with a 5 per cent Black population. Indian residents constituted 1.5 per cent and Pakistani 1.4 per cent of the local population. However, despite fairly similar representations of minority ethnic people in the area – George Park – as with the area described above, this school had a larger number of minority ethnic pupils than School A. Nine per cent of the school population were African-

Caribbean and 12 per cent of pupils were Asian. White pupils constituted 78 per cent of the school population. School B also took a large number of pupils excluded from the nearby technology school (see School C below) as both schools were in close proximity. It was therefore for some students either a second choice school, as the waiting list for School C was fairly long, or a school attended by those unable to remain within the school of their original choice.

In a school with approximately 675 students, there were 115 exclusions. Of all exclusions 35.6 per cent were of African-Caribbean pupils. Of these 33 per cent were of African-Caribbean boys who constituted only 6 per cent of the school population. In the year in which research took place a new discipline policy meant that exclusions increased. In the first term and a half of the new policy coming into force, there were 109 exclusions of which 4 were permanent. This is a considerable number given the total of 115 exclusions which had taken place in the previous academic year. In the first term alone 37 per cent of the exclusions were given to Black pupils who constituted 12 per cent of the school population. The reasons for the majority of these exclusions included verbal abuse and disruptive behaviour.

There was a greater focus on 'race' as illustrated by a number of displays on the walls. There was also quite a high focus on discipline within the school. School B had recently introduced a new exclusion policy based on advice given to them by an inspector the previous year. This policy was based on what a senior staff member referred to as 'zero tolerance' and involved quicker recourse to the use of fixed period exclusion. Children would be reprimanded three times and at the third time would be issued with a slip. If a child received a slip they would be told to spend time in the on-site unit. Receipt of three slips resulted in a fixed period exclusion. Exclusion rates were therefore quite high, although the Headteacher expected that these would soon level off. The exclusions of Black pupils, however, remained relatively high and the pupils who had experienced exclusion spoke of the existence of tensions between them and senior members of staff. A Black parent support group met regularly at the school with the support of Section 11 staff. Many of them also voiced concern about the school's new discipline policy, especially in relation to Black children. Children from all ethnic groups interviewed said that the process leading to an exclusion was rapid. Pupils complained that even when they wanted to complain that they had not been responsible for a specific behaviour resulting in a warning, they would receive another slip simply for speaking out in the classroom and making that response. School B was also under local authority control.

School C

School C was a new technology school of eight years at the time of research, located in the centre of the city. The area in which the school was situated –

George Park – was as previously mentioned, mainly White, although this school was situated close to a more affluent area of the city where staff from the local university and many other professionals lived. However, School C was also close to areas in receipt of City Challenge funding.[1] School C had a remit to enrol potential pupils living in local inner city areas only. These areas included places with a higher than local average proportion of minority ethnic residents. Attending pupils lived in, for example Hightown, where Black residents constituted 13.7 per cent of the local population; Lee Park, where Black residents made up 8.8 per cent and Pakistani residents 7.4 per cent of the local area, and Crest Hill where Black residents constituted 6.9 per cent of the local population and Pakistani at a high 15.2 per cent. During the research the school widened the catchment area to include all of the city in view of its increasing popularity among local families.

The school had quite high proportions of African-Caribbean and Asian students and was very well resourced. Asian pupils, with a high proportion of Pakistani students, constituted 20 per cent of the pupil population. Ten per cent of pupils were African-Caribbean and only 58 per cent of pupils were White. It had strong links with the local business community and the proportion of pupils achieving GCSE grade A–Cs had recently begun to increase. The school, however, had developed a reputation among local Black voluntary organizations for excluding large numbers of Black pupils. Despite this, many Black parents placed their children's names on the school waiting list because of the high achievement rate and the obvious advantage School C had over other maintained schools in relation to resources.

Senior staff were clear that the exclusions had reduced in recent years. In a school of 782 pupils there were 43 exclusions. However 37.2 per cent of all exclusions were of African-Caribbean pupils, with 44 per cent of permanent exclusions affecting this group in particular. African-Caribbean boys, one of the smallest minority ethnic groups in the school, constituted 5 per cent of the pupil population, yet 21 per cent of all exclusions were of African-Caribbean males.

The majority of staff at the school were young or newly qualified teachers and the last inspection report for the school commented on the lack of adequate support networks for these particular teachers. It had also been noted by inspectors that pupils were not given enough help so that they could conduct work independently. The school had developed a strong link with a local Black voluntary association and an educational programme had recently been set up to assist with the achievement of African and African-Caribbean pupils. The discipline policy for the school was only available in draft form and thus there were no clear guidelines for defusing misbehaviour. All senior staff saw the use of school exclusion as inevitable, but did not think that ultimately exclusion solved the problems for the pupil. At the time of the research there was no formal discipline policy. There was no consistency in relation to particular offences and the sanctions required. The issue of inconsistency was reflected by permanent excludees from the school, featured later in the book, who complained about insufficient notice of an exclusion and the fact that necessary documentation relating to an exclusion was often unavailable.

School D

School D was situated on the border of two very different parts of the city. One of these had a large number of local authority housing estates and pockets of disadvantage, whilst the other had a larger proportion of privately owned homes and was not as ethnically diverse. High Town had the highest proportion of Black residents in the city at 13.7 per cent whereas Lake Park contained wealthier residents, 93.5 per cent of whom were White. The school, however, drew the majority of its pupil population from High Town and would frequently receive pupils excluded from elsewhere. In particular the Headteacher had complained that some children would begin attending the school for the first few years, and then leave to attend School C once a place there became available. What the Head found particularly problematic was the increasing number of pupils who had started off at her school in Year 7, gone to attend School C, and returned again to her school having experienced an exclusion. These children she pointed out were for the most part African-Caribbean and male.

The school had a large amount of children with an emotional and/or behavioural difficulty and their GCSE results had been lower than both local and national averages.

Twenty-three per cent of all pupils at School D were African-Caribbean with 10 per cent Asian. However the rates of exclusion for Black children were high. Thirty-eight per cent of fixed period exclusions were of African-Caribbean pupils, and out of four permanent exclusions, two were of African-Caribbean boys.

The school had recently introduced a new exclusion policy through which the Headteacher wanted to draw out the small minority of pupils who were constantly given a variety of school sanctions. The Headteacher tried to avoid using both fixed period and permanent exclusions as much as possible, but found that keeping particular pupils within school was detrimental to some pupils and staff. None the less the school tended to retain pupils for longer than did most others. Because of this, there was concern that many pupils excluded from other schools would be told by the local education department to apply to School D. Within the school, however, there was a much larger focus than the other participating schools on the rewarding of good behaviour. Much of this reward policy was featured in the school prospectus, which interestingly contrasted with the focus on discipline and the new exclusion policy featured on the front page of the prospectus for School B. In line with many of the efforts by senior staff to avoid exclusion wherever possible, an inspection report for the school noted that there was a caring atmosphere within the school, and a group of staff committed to raising achievement.

School E

School E was situated in the centre of a large mainly White working-class housing estate and had recently attained grant maintained status. Old Town comprised 91.8 per cent White residents, 4.3 per cent Black and 2.2 per cent Indian. However in the surrounding estate White residents constituted 95.6 per cent and Black residents 3.4 per cent of the population. There were no significant Asian residents in the area which contributed to the racial harassment suffered by those Asian residents who had remained. The school had been due to close because of falling rolls, but parents and local community members had wanted the school to remain open and the Head had decided to apply for grant maintained status. During the time in which the decision to grant this status was being made the possibility of closure remained. The rolls had fallen lower. Consequently many potential students chose to go elsewhere. The school therefore had a very small number of students attending and there were very few ethnic minority pupils.

Within the housing estate served by the school there are very few ethnic minority residents and teachers within the school commented on the racial tension experienced by the few African-Caribbean families who did live in the area. The majority of Asian families who had once settled on the estate had been driven out of the area by some White residents.

Within the school there were no Asian students and African-Caribbean/ mixed parentage students constituted 1 per cent of the pupil population. However, 2.7 per cent of all exclusions were of African-Caribbean boys – no Black girls were excluded. Out of a school with only 302 pupils, 73 exclusions were given which constitutes the highest rate out of all the schools researched.

There was a heavier focus on attendance at School E than in any of the other participating schools. Though the school had a rewards and sanctions policy, the process for the imposing of sanctions on pupils was not clear and appeared to be at the discretion of individual staff. However there was also a clear focus on rewards, and full attendance would be rewarded both termly and yearly. Monetary awards for improved or full attendance were common. After an inspection which took place during the period in which the research was conducted, it was recommended that the school should be placed on special measures.

Opinions on Exclusion: Inclusive and Exclusive School Cultures

Writers such as Peters and Waterman (1982) suggest that successful organizations have appropriate, strong and coherent organizational cultures, which take account of diversity. At school level Headteachers offer the most important lead, which can make a difference at an institutional level. They have a vital role to play in developing inclusive whole school policies, which are coherent and consistently applied, thus reducing disaffection and disruptive behaviour. The Headteacher who makes the ultimate decision to exclude is one of the most important individuals in the exclusion process. Research on good practice in the area of exclusions notes that leadership from both the Headteacher and the senior management team is essential in creating an ethos within which exclusion and discipline is adequately and consistently managed (Osler 1997: 73; Benson 1996).

Some of the senior staff and subject teachers within the participating schools spoke about the issue of exclusion in terms of a dichotomy between the challenging few and the well-behaved majority. This discourse which was used as a justification for using exclusion as a sanction, depended upon the type of ethos promoted within the school. The dichotomy between the badly and well behaved was further situated within the educational debates surrounding pupil disruption. This particular view of the use of exclusion characterized much of the previous government's approach to the issue of pupil disruption and was further situated within notions of declining morality, lack of parental control and the 'yobbo' culture. Through educational policy emphases on competition between schools, the challenging few have become a group of individuals likely not only to damage the educational chances of other more well-behaved pupils, but in doing so they are seen as adversely affecting the ability of the school to attract more desirable pupils. In this respect the response to the disruptive minority can be likened to historical perceptions of particular deviant groups, who, in relation to lack of income, criminal behaviour, sexual orientation or ethnic background, 'contaminate' the law abiding, societal majority.

Out of all the senior staff interviewed, the Headteacher of School B talked most frequently about protecting the well-behaved majority, in order to justify his high fixed-term exclusion rate. His decision to publicize his new discipline policy in the school prospectus constructed a particular image of the school for new and potential students and parents. Discipline was clearly central to the ethos of the school, and his concern only to educate the well-behaved majority was the main focus of the new discipline policy. He had no concerns for the pupils whom he felt were badly behaved:

> 'I hope the exclusions will go down as pupils adjust to stricter regimes and knowing that the rules are tight, but even if they didn't, I would still feel that it is much better this way round. And the exclusion of those pupils is a price to be paid for better discipline in the school so the majority can learn effectively.'
>
> (Mr Mills, Headteacher, School B)

For Mr Mills, exclusion was not only a means of setting an example to all pupils around the boundaries of acceptable behaviour. Although he had introduced the policy in order that pupils would be aware that behaviour needed to improve, he also states that the exclusion of badly behaved pupils is a price that the school could pay in order to maintain the majority. In placing the minority of pupils upon this particular boundary, it is clear that should he need to exclude permanently all of those pupils in the minority, it is an action he is prepared to take.

Other senior teachers spoke in similar ways in terms of protecting the well-behaved majority. In some cases their emphasis was more on setting boundaries in order to retain those pupils within the school, rather than as a means of sifting out those who were undesirable. Again the process of differentiating between good and bad pupils was dependent upon the type of school and the place of discipline within the overall school ethos. For School B discipline and hence exclusion had become quite central. Many children within the catchment area of the school had elected to attend School C for a variety of reasons and the school did not have a comprehensive pupil intake. Many pupils attending in Year 7 had poor literacy skills. The Head, though welcoming the diversity of his pupil intake, also saw it as challenging, and had expressed concern about the parental backgrounds of many of his pupils. He felt that in some cases where children lived with a lone parent, this was significant in their behaviour at school. However, in School D, where a high proportion of pupils were African-Caribbean and many pupils were living in lone parent families, the distinction made between the well-behaved majority and the challenging minority was based on a need to support the minority.

The school had also lost many of its prospective, and at times attending, pupils to School C. Concurrently, it had taken on many pupils with emotional and behavioural difficulties, as well as those with poor literacy skills. The Head, and many of her senior staff recognized that this support for the challenging minority, unfortunately took place at the expense of the more well behaved, but felt that high exclusions of pupils did not solve the problem.

> 'If we're saying that schools are about giving children maximum opportunities for their potential, we actually haven't got room for severely disruptive pupils and those two – they're both boys – those two boys are severely disrupting the learning of pupils. And I just think that's happening more because whilst we're doing what we can for the minority, the challenging few – and we do do a lot for them – you can't allow them to affect the learning of so many others. We've got an increasing number of children who are EBD. So it's getting quite hair-raising now, with the number of EBD children that we're having to deal with and I have to find a fair and efficient and practical way of making sure that we do everything we possibly can to support.'
>
> (Mrs Ardle, Headteacher, School D)

Though the views around disruptive pupils expressed here by the Head of School D are similar to those of Mr Mills above, Mrs Ardle looked at the issue of exclusion as a sanction to be used only in the absence of any alternative. It is also possible to interpret Mrs Ardle's view as one of 'survival' – School D was rapidly being given the status of a 'sink school', and the local education authority regularly recommended that pupils excluded from elsewhere approach the school for admission. Many of the senior staff at School D, recognizing the increasing difficulty they were experiencing in encouraging prospective pupils to attend, favoured the minority versus majority view in support of exclusions:

> 'I think we under-exclude. I think because we understand it we deal with it. We actually have some children here who are putting other children off coming. I think by trying to help them and trying to deal with them we actually cut our own throats to some extent.'
>
> (Mrs Dougal, Head of Year, School D)

There was also an awareness that the reputation the school had gained over the years, both within the local community and the education department, was one in which the identity of the excludee had become racialized. Using the minority versus majority view to discuss the issue of exclusions, however, did not simply mean that the school wished to encourage the admission of well-behaved White students at the expense of disruptive Black pupils. Rather the school recognized that many of the Black children currently attending were achieving relatively well, and had become part of the majority group that senior teachers wished to protect:

> 'What has happened recently is that we've had a high proportion of requests to admit African-Caribbean boys who had been permanently excluded from elsewhere, by area office. But I think two things were happening. Firstly [their] parents would think "well there are a lot of African-Caribbean kids here, that could be a good place for them to be". But of course what was happening was we were getting a dis-proportionate number of requests and if you keep including poor role models for Black kids who are doing well ... Basically it's a racist move to be honest and I suppose people do it with good intent. But we've taken a stand on that.'
>
> (Mrs Roberts, Deputy Head, School D)

In comparison, Mr Mills wanted all potentially disruptive pupils to be aware that his new discipline policy meant that it was unlikely that they would receive any support from staff. Rather than using fixed-term exclusion as a last resort, he requested that all staff employ a set procedure using the issuing of specific warnings should a child become disruptive. Once a child was involved in the disciplinary procedure, staff were instructed not to offer counsel to pupils, or to enquire what was encouraging particular forms of behaviour. In his report to the school governors, Mr Mills stated that less time would now be spent with parents at exclusions meetings and that they would not be given the opportunity to question the validity of exclusion decisions. If a parent rang to complain about a decision made to exclude their child, staff were instructed to make excuses on the telephone in order to terminate the conversation.

'I think the support should be there so long as they are behaving well. People go out of their way to talk to them and see how they're getting on and the care should be whilst they're behaving well. Once they start to behave badly that's it. A lot of people who get themselves into trouble is attention seeking behaviour and then what used to happen was they'd get even more attention because teachers spend a lot of time talking to the pupil, counselling and so on. So they begin to associate "let's misbehave, you get more attention". So what we're trying to do is break that link and say if you don't behave you won't get any attention.'

(Mr Mills, Headteacher, School D)

Mr Mills did not want to explore why particular children may have been seeking particular forms of attention. Clearly if there were extenuating factors which encouraged certain forms of behaviour in children, such as finding work difficult, simple, tedious or the possibility that conflict might exist between pupils and teachers/peers, then these issues were not to be resolved within school. The documentation relating to exclusions would also now be reduced. No witness statements from other members of staff would now be required and in some cases a single senior teacher would be allowed to make recommendations to exclude simply on the basis of what they had seen. Mr Mills recognized the difficulties which could arise should a multitude of fixed-term exclusions for a child lead to a permanent exclusion, particularly if no documentation was available. Mr Mills recommended to staff and governors that proper judgement would need to be taken in instances where teachers felt that a temporary exclusion received by a particular pupil was likely to result in permanent exclusion for which documentation would be required. In that instance, documentation would need to be prepared in anticipation of this occurrence. There were a plethora of issues relating to staff accountability, consistency of approach within the policy, and the preparation of documents *only* in situations where public scrutiny may be a possibility.

Mr Mills was very keen that the GCSE results for the school improve, and often the extenuating circumstances of many of the children who were giving staff cause for concern, became subsumed within more academic concerns. His staff welcomed the structure that the new discipline policy brought to the issue of pastoral care, but were also concerned about the reasons behind disruptive behaviour:

'There's no feeling like it when you see these children and you let go. You know what sort of road they are going to go down, and I feel absolutely powerless. The kids bring so much baggage with them but you can't because you've got so many children in the school. As head of year I have recommended lots of children to be excluded. Not easily. It's not something I do lightly. You recommend them to be excluded if they break certain guidelines. *We have a list of guidelines so it is largely taken out of our hands.'*

(Mrs Clare, Assistant Deputy Head, School D)

It has been suggested that discipline policies should lay out structures to support staff but should not be so prescriptive as to encourage the possibility of excluding pupils for whom such a sanction is not appropriate (Osler 1997). Mrs Clare, above, had an increasingly demanding role as a Head of Year, Head of Language Department and assistant to the Deputy Head. However, her role also meant that she knew a lot of information about the children who would be recommended for exclusion and her final comment in relation to the new guidelines is particularly revealing. The new disciplinary policy adopted at School B was quite heavily prescriptive, as the Headteacher felt such strict guidelines were necessary in order to provide support to staff. However the nature of these guidelines was not always appropriate:

'People have got to work within the system. I think that if you actually try and do things your own way and undermine the school policy then it creates a lot of difficulty. I think there are some times when you know that something has gone on with an individual pupil, or you know about the background of the pupil [and] a lot of people would say we should have a consistent policy. I think by and large we do try but we have individual cases where you know that the worst possible thing for that child would be an exclusion, because of the home circumstances and what will happen if that pupil is excluded. With people like that you do hold back and I think that's where schools get themselves into difficulties and people say this should have happened, but you are really trying to protect that child.'

(Ms Reid, Senior Support/Guidance Teacher, School B)

Ms Reid, along with many of the senior management staff at School B, felt that the new policy was useful and much time was being spent encouraging all staff to use it well. However, she has also noted that the structures embedded within the policy do not always fit with all pupils. Consistent approaches to school exclusion and other sanctions are desirable within a majority of schools and it is recommended that offences, and their corresponding sanctions, be listed in school discipline policies (Social Exclusion Unit 1998). However, it is clear that often such consistency is difficult to achieve. Furthermore, such a perspective assumes that all pupils misbehave for similar reasons regardless of particular circumstances, and as became evident within School B, that particular groups of pupils may be more likely to experience sanctions.

The ways in which senior staff view their disruptive minority can provide an interesting starting point to understanding school ethos. School B wanted to concentrate on the well-behaved majority – as indeed do many schools –

but in doing so appeared to disregard the nature of their pupil intake and some of the difficulties behind particular forms of behaviour. School D on the other hand, recognized that far too much time was spent on the minority who misbehaved. However, in acknowledging the nature of their pupil intake, the Head and the senior teachers were reluctant to adopt a policy which disregarded extenuating circumstance. It is possible to look at School B as also enacting a survivalist strategy – teachers here were aware of the difficulties experienced by staff and pupils at School D and in believing them to be more extreme, did not want to see a similar situation develop in their own school. However, other less senior members of staff at School B did not have as much faith in the leadership of the Headteacher, and hence many of the policies he developed. Conflicting views on the nature of adequate forms of discipline and staff perceptions of badly behaved pupils, can create an ethos where pupils and staff are unsure about the boundaries. Not only this, but where conflicting staff interpretations of discipline become obvious to pupils, they may be more likely to view boundaries set by staff as invalid. This problem can be particularly acute where the school has attempted to introduce a new, consistent policy, whilst also allowing for particular exceptions to the rule.

The Concept of Punishment

Within all staff perceptions of adequate discipline will lie particular beliefs about the nature and function of punishment. The term punishment itself can conjure up images of physical restraint, and though corporal punishment in state schools has been illegal since 1987, some of the older teachers in the schools remembered and greatly valued the use of caning. Present debates about physical punishment have been extended to include parents and childminders, and critics of this form of discipline have asserted that children should have the same rights against physical assault as adults (*The Guardian*, 1998). Exclusion has always been the last resort for schools but with the removal of corporal punishment, and in the absence of such a physical alternative, some teachers continue to believe that children deserve to be *punished* for bad behaviour. The competing visions of childhood and adulthood that such understandings of punishment conjure up reflect wider opinion that societal mores have diminished and that particular groups of children and their families require harsher societal sanctions. For example, there has been increasing government pressure to fine the families of repeat juvenile offenders, and to introduce harsher penalties for the young offenders themselves. This was also reflected in governmental fears of what they perceived to be the increasing British 'yob' culture, and escalating degrees of soccer hooliganism. This was seen as partially responsible for the increasing exclusion and underachievement of boys at school.

The notion of punishment within schools reflects the age and hence power related differentials which exist between adult and child. Discourses around school exclusions and the host of other sanctions currently available to schools, create an image of punishment which is used to teach particular lessons, frighten children into submission, correct irresponsible immature behaviours and ultimately prevent the recurrence of poor behaviour. These images of punishment in sanctioning an individual, reinforce the view that the offender is answerable to others. Thus, whereas a pupil may achieve temporary power over a peer or teacher when involved in confrontation, the use of school sanction to punish the pupil, asserts the power and authority of the teacher/adult over the pupil/child. School-based punishment in reinforcing the position of the pupil in relation to his or her age, has implications for adolescence. Punishment itself is a problematic concept, particularly for older school children. The majority of exclusions occur in key Stage 4 which is a particularly crucial time for young people educationally. It is also at this time that many begin to find the use of school exclusion, or more importantly, the concept of being 'punished' quite patronizing. The concept of punishment can, therefore, produce pupil responses which are not conducive to the forging of positive teacher–pupil relationships. Some teachers within the case study schools currently complain that, in order to prevent indiscipline, sanctions should be preventative and harsh enough for 'lesson learning'. However a focus on harshness will not necessarily change pupil behaviour.

> 'Punishment ... has the propensity to deter, to reinforce the importance of school rules and teacher expectations, and to prompt culprits to see the error of their ways. But unless administered sensitively, it can alienate, reinforce attention seeking behaviour, encourage avoidance tactics, induce feelings of rejection, and, if severe, expose pupils to inappropriate adult models whose aggression might be imitated.'
>
> (Docking 1987: 19)

However, as will be shown in later chapters, particular associations of punishment with masculinity by teaching staff, created a school ethos within which constructs of retribution, revenge and violence permeated the language of male pupils.

Definitions of punishment are clearly embedded within teacher opinions on the function of school sanction. The Head of School D believed fixed-term exclusions were useful as a defuser rather than as a punishment. Other senior teachers saw fixed-term exclusion as allowing a breathing space for pupils or staff. Whichever discourse was used by teachers to define exclusion, the rationale behind all sanctions was to reinforce to pupils the fact that specific lines of authority existed within school. For those senior teachers who were quite clear about the reasons for retaining the use of school exclusion – as a means of reinforcing teacher/school authority – this would be reflected in their exclusion rate. Thus the Headteacher of School B who felt it necessary to use a stricter discipline policy had a fairly high rate of exclusions. In the first term and a half that the new discipline policy had come into effect, over one hundred fixed-term and permanent exclusions had taken place with a disproportionate number affecting African-Caribbean students. The exclusion rate for School E had placed it in the top 20 per cent of similar schools with high exclusion figures, yet the Headteacher maintained that such a high rate of exclusions was necessary as part of an overall focus on behaviour management. The pupils at School E, and the communities from which they were drawn, had developed particular reputations over the years for anti-social behaviour. Thus the Head saw it as necessary that the disciplinary policy within the school should reflect those levels of behaviour.

However within other participating schools teacher opinions about the nature and function of punishment were not simplistically reflected in their exclusion statistics. In School A, for example, the Deputy Headteacher who was for the most part solely responsible for all pastoral issues, was adamant that exclusions were inevitable, and though there had only been five permanent exclusions in the 12 years that he had been in post, he felt that the fixed-term exclusions were high. As an African-Caribbean senior member of staff, he distinguished between the disciplinary practices he adopted and those of some of the older Caribbean parents of children at the school, which he likened to 'fire and brimstone'. Yet he was fairly strict and consistent in his use of discipline. Nevertheless, in comparison to other similar schools, the exclusion rate for School A was low. The fact that there had been very few permanent exclusions from the school was a clear indication that the children were more likely to be maintained within it. This transmits particular messages both to pupils and parents about the ethos of the school, and though there were clearly tensions which existed between many of the excludees and members of staff (see Chapters 4 and 5), the overall academic achievements of pupils were extremely high.

The Headteacher of School C, on the other hand, also saw exclusions as 'inevitable', but had taken many steps to reduce the number of fixed-term exclusions.

'I'd like to get to the state where we use it [exclusions] so infrequently that it's a really rare occurrence. Inevitably in the sort of society we live in you need sanctions. I would hope that long term we motivate children so much that we don't have to use exclusions at all. Maybe the odd day or half day because young people do daft things sometimes and you need to make sure that they learn from their mistakes. So you have to use something, but we do things like Saturday detentions instead, so there are other options. Punishment really isn't a very useful concept. We all want the same things, including the children. Sometimes they do things they regret and you have to enable them to learn from that and mature and grow up. I would hope that all the sanctions we take are aimed at that, not just making the kid feel bad. That doesn't achieve anything.'

(Mrs Clements, Headteacher, School C)

This Headteacher talked about sanctions as a means through which the pupils could learn from their mistakes, and saw the concept of punishment itself as unhelpful. She also saw exclusions in a similar way to achievement – the achievement figures for both GCSE and A levels had improved steadily over the years, and she now wanted to see the exclusion figures reduced significantly. Thus the school held Saturday detentions for disruptive pupils, and the Headteacher had encouraged all staff to praise pupils wherever possible, so avoiding confrontation. However, the school had developed a particular reputation among Black parents and local community organizations for disproportionate exclusions of African-Caribbean pupils and some parents within the community remained suspicious of the school. In addition to this, teachers in School D commented on the number of their pupils who had once attended School C and had been asked to move. As the Headteacher herself suggested:

> 'Sometimes it's entirely appropriate to negotiate a move because for some reason a child hasn't settled, something else would be more appropriate and they can move on without stigma.'
>
> (Mrs Clements, Headteacher, School C)

Thus in this respect the decreasing exclusion figures that School C was enjoying had been influenced by parents agreeing to send their children to other schools, and it is important that the Headteacher's progressive views on punishment be set within this context. However it is also worth noting that many of the strategies adopted within the school – for example making sure that young people were referred to as 'students' and allowing them to use the school premises quite freely at break and lunchtimes – also reflected many of the Headteacher's views on the nature of school sanctions. Whereas discipline had been quite central to the overall ethos of the school a few years prior to the research, the Headteacher saw this as an aside to the importance of academic achievement. In a similar way to the Headteacher of School A, who had delegated all responsibility for discipline to her Deputy Head, Mrs Clements wanted to concentrate on managing the image of the school through attracting the interests of local businesses and ensuring that the school be placed favourably in the league tables. Discipline, punishment and school sanctions had become more of an 'irritation' than a central aspect of schooling young people.

Much of the conflict between the progressive notions around discipline, childhood and education embedded within School C and the experiences of the Black children within, were very closely related to its position as a specialist school. As technology and specialist schools continue to increase, the implications of a business-oriented curriculum and the wider definitions of schooling young people are greater for those who may not be identified as able to compete adequately and hence survive in the marketplace. Quite clearly there are at least two cultures operating within the school, the dominant one which is schooling–business-oriented and the sub-cultures of some minority ethnic students which demand respect from all members of the organization. The second is destined for confrontation with the first given the managerialist stance of the school. Most importantly it is notable that there needs to be a good fit between the context and the culture of the organization if an organization is to achieve success. If one looks at specialist and technology schools there are immediate causes for concern, most of which arise from the fit between the values/culture of business and the self-professed values of education. As described by two young people who had at different times experienced a permanent exclusion from School C:

> School B is a normal school. School C is not normal. The teachers are not normal and the pupils are not normal.
> (Stephen, aged 16, permanently excluded from School C)

> At CTC they treat you like you're in a prison. If you want to go anywhere you can't get there or get anything without your card.
> (Chris, aged 16, permanently excluded from School C)

Thus some technology and indeed grant maintained schools may be in danger of moving away from the socio-developmental needs of the children on the development road into adulthood. One example of this is the inability at the governor level to provide the flexibility that the pupils need to learn from their mistakes and to reach their wider social and corresponding educational potential. It is unlikely that business sector governors will be as aware of the needs of their young charges as ordinary parent governors.

Technology/specialist schools tend to be well-resourced establishments and many students do indeed benefit from the opportunities they offer, most particularly the new and exciting curriculum and the important links with businesses. However Black parents must be warned that the vulnerability of Black students to exclusion has particularly severe consequences. Once excluded, students' immediate educational careers are endangered because they are unlikely to get into a school which will extend to them the same specialist curriculum offered by the technology school. They may have only a few brief years or months to catch up on a new curriculum, and may have to wait until college to pick up their earlier scientific and technological areas of interest.

Conclusion

The ethos of a school can often embody a complex variety of educational, pastoral, familial and disciplinary discourses. Children in schools and indeed their parents expect that pupils will be taught and will achieve their full potential. Teachers expect to be able to concentrate on the delivery of their subjects within an environment which will be educationally stimulating, positive, caring and structured. It is at the point where structures break down that the caring, stimulating and positive ethos which encourages a learning atmosphere is at odds with the assertion of authority and the reinforcement of teacher–pupil boundaries which is at the basis of discipline. Disicpline aims to reinforce the structures which have broken down. The notion that children are punished 'for their own good' integrates the negative ways in which discipline is enforced and received, with the assumption that it will have a positive outcome for the young person. The contradiction embedded within this and the ethos of educating in a caring yet structured/disciplined way is difficult to overcome for many young people, as well as some of the teachers.

Although exclusions are increasing within primary schools, many of the problems which arise out of the contradictions between care and control are quite specific to the secondary sector. The rapid approach to adulthood of many young people of secondary school age disrupts the way in which such positive and negative constructs have co-existed in primary education. The ways that some of the older teachers in the schools spoke about the lack of alternatives to caning, and their frustration at having to rely simply on exclusions from school, reflected a definition of punishment as a means of frightening pupils into submission. Such understandings of punishment imply that childhood is an age period extending often up to and beyond the age of 16, which is at odds with the increasing maturity of even young teenagers. It is necessary for schools to transmit a climate of justice within their overall ethos in order to overcome some of the contradictions embedded within them. Where young people feel sanctions are imposed equitably, they are likely to encourage their use where necessary (Osler 1997; Weekes and Wright 1996).

It is also clear that at the basis of school approaches to exclusion were particular conceptions of pupils. It has been suggested that a school's 'true threshold of tolerance' can be measured against the numbers of children they permanently exclude (McManus 1987: 26). Indeed the tolerance level appears to relate to teacher opinion of the types of pupil they teach. The senior teachers featured within this chapter had a variety of definitions of the child/young person and the dichotomy between the well-behaved majority as opposed to the poorly behaved minority, also translates into a perception that there are simply small numbers of children who are beyond help. Where schools are not in a constructive dialogue with other agencies, such definitions of the child and the threshold of tolerance which emerges from this, creates a climate and cycle of conflict which, as will be shown, has great implications for the educational lives of young Black students.

Note

1 City Challenge included money set aside by government for the regeneration of areas deprived in relation to housing, rates of unemployment, etc.

3   Teachers and Pupils – Relationships of Power and Resistance

Introduction

Pupil resistance within schools has long been theorized and debated within the sociology of education. Theories on the relationship between pupil and school have historically argued that schools are quite clearly implicated in the reproduction of social divisions (Bowles and Gintis 1976), but were criticized for suggesting that schools could not make a difference to the creating of inequalities among pupils (McFadden 1995). Resistance theories thus have emerged in response to the often deterministic analyses embedded within social reproduction theories and have looked at the possibility of schools creating agents who can, through various forms of cultural resistance, effect changes within oppressive social structures (Giroux 1983). The tension between structure and agency that such work has thrown up, has avoided the determinism which results from giving social structures a form of 'intentional rationality'. Instead, resistance theory has looked at the limits of these structures, through examining the agency of disadvantaged pupils who reject what educational institutions have to offer. However, resistance theories themselves have also been the subject of theoretical and empirical criticism since the mid-1980s. Much of this has focused on the gendered romanticism used to understand working-class male youth (McRobbie 1978), and the failure of such theories to examine the areas where class specific forms of resistance intersect with social relations of 'race', gender and sexuality (Watson 1993; Meyenn 1980; Walker 1986; Mac an Ghaill 1988, 1994). In view of these, there has been an increasing body of work conducted by feminists on gendered forms of resistance and the implications of these for masculine and feminine identities (Davies 1984; Anyon 1983; Riddell 1989), and by researchers on the resistances of Black pupils in schools (Mac an Ghaill 1988; Gillborn 1990; Sewell 1997; Wright 1985, 1992). Much of this work, however, has also been subjected to theoretical and methodological criticism, which has moved the debate on race and gender within education beyond the sphere of schooling, and into wider discussions as to the nature of institutionalized sexism and racism (Hammersley and Gomm 1993; Foster et al. 1996). There are problems surrounding the definition of all forms of oppositional behaviour in schools as resistant (Brittan and Maynard 1984), and all too often theories of resistance provide inadequate strategies for change (Gewirz 1991). Despite this, it will be argued here that the theorizing of pupil behaviour within the area of resistance and/or contestation continues to be theoretically important. In order to explore the relevance of theorizing pupil resistance, particularly in relation to the experience of school, the responses to schooling of African-Caribbean and Asian pupils will be explored. Though much research has highlighted the processes through which Black pupils resist education (Mac an Ghaill 1988; Cashmore and Troyna 1982), the relationship between racialized strategies of resisting teacher authority, and the power embedded within the sanction of school exclusion remains unexplored. It is important therefore to examine whether the sanction of school exclusion reflects the relationship between pupil as resister/contester and the powers held by schools to exclude and/or the powers of teachers to employ school sanctions as a response to pupil resistance. Notions of resistance in relation to the racialized positions of African-Caribbean and Asian pupils and excludees, and their often conflictual relationships with teachers and schools will be interrogated. In this way it will be possible to examine whether racializing the concept of 'resistance' within the context of school exclusion, can adequately reflect the experiences of these children both whilst within, and excluded from, the education institution.

Understanding 'Resistance'

The concept of 'resistance' in relation to schooling has been employed by a number of writers keen to explore how specific groups of pupils negotiate and respond to their marginal positions in schools, whilst avoiding a determinist analysis of schools' ability to reproduce these social and cultural inequalities. The seminal work of Paul Willis (1977) attempted to interrogate the division between structure and agency that earlier social reproduction accounts had introduced. Through suggesting that the resistance of the working-class males in his study acted to reinforce their social class positions, Willis argued that this was a choice his participants actively made. In this way he attempted to engage debate on the issue of structure and agency. However, Willis's work has been criticized as dualistic and determinist (Walker 1986). It has been suggested that though Willis wished to avoid a determinist analysis through giving the 'lads' agency, he posited an image of working-class culture as oppressive. Though feminists attacked Willis's work for its over-romanticized view of working-class masculinity (McRobbie 1991), their own work on female resistance also acted to cement the lives of their respondents in working-class culture, albeit through their respondents' own choosing (McRobbie 1978; Anyon 1983; Davies 1983). The term 'resistance within accommodation' has been used by feminist researchers to suggest that young women strategically employ aspects of exaggerated femininity in schools, such as blushing and giggling with (male) teachers, in order to avoid work. In this way it is argued, young women effect forms of resistance within the context of the classroom and the teacher–pupil relationship. However, often the issue of what is specifically being resisted by pupils becomes more complex, where theorists' assume that the exaggeration of femininity described above can be seen as a rejection of the norms of femininity (Gewirz 1991). The problems relating to structure and agency within resistance theories were therefore closely related to their emphasis on social reproduction. Critics suggested that though resistance theories were ideally placed to explore pupils' responses to schooling (Sultana 1989), they continued to focus on students' rejection of social structures. As McFadden (1995) has argued:

> disadvantage and inequality of achievement at school is related more to the rejection of the curriculum and pedagogy encountered by students than to a conscious resistance to the dominant ideology of society.
>
> (McFadden 1995: 297)

Therefore research on resistance has led to alternative interpretations of pupil responses to schooling. Some writers have argued that resistance to schooling is not restricted to that of working-class pupils (Aggleton 1987; Watson 1993) and indeed that some resistance may not be particularly class based (Meyenn 1980). Other research, particularly in the area of 'race', has shown that African Caribbean pupils, particularly males, exhibit pro-school as well as anti-school attitudes (Gillborn 1990; Sewell 1996). This is particularly important as much educational research conducted on Black pupils in British schools has focused on disaffection (Mac an Ghaill 1988; Cashmore and Troyna 1982). Another important aspect not restricted to 'race', but which has certain 'race'-specific connotations, is that contrary to the basis of earlier resistance theories, many pupils do not reject the concept of education itself, but rather the authoritarian function of teachers (Mac an Ghaill 1994) and the form and content of the curriculum. Research has also indicated that many Black pupils do recognize the value of education but reject the wider racialized and gendered discrimination which filters through into perceptions of their behaviour by peers and teachers (Fuller 1982). Therefore McFadden (1995) argues that resistance theory needs to account for the variety in pupil responses to schooling which may be mediated through class, gender and 'race' and the importance of the intersection between pupil and teacher perceptions. It is also important to view the resistances of pupils as a response to the nature of knowledge which they receive in schools. He suggests that

> students from certain kinds of backgrounds have experiences of schooling which restrict their opportunity to extend their knowledge. The response to this form of schooling for many students is to resist it.

> What students are constantly rejecting, or sometimes at best, merely
> complying with regardless of class, gender, race and ethnicity, is
> schooling which depowers them.
>
> (McFadden 1995: 297)

Research on 'race' and resistance within schooling has been subject to
criticism which suggests that it is difficult both to distinguish between pupil
resistance and simple 'messing about' (Brittan and Maynard 1984; Gewirz
1991), and to 'prove' empirically that the teacher racism against which the
majority of anti-school Black pupils resist, actually exists (Foster 1990,
1991; Hammersley and Gomm 1993). In a similar form to the criticism
levelled at feminist theorizing of 'resistance within accommodation', the
nature of the criticism directed at much research on 'race' has suggested that
Black pupils merely reinforce dominant racialized stereotypes (Gewirz 1991;
Foster et al. 1996). For example, theorists on race and educational inequality
have suggested that Black pupils exhibit particular forms of speech (Mac an
Ghaill 1988), ways of walking (Gillborn 1990), and more recently types of
dress (Sewell 1997), which are indicative of pupil resistance. Foster et al.
(1996) argue that these explanations of pupil behaviour are culturally
essentialist as reducing forms of behaviour to 'race' also ignores the effect of
class and gender on behaviour. Foster et al. (1996) use this critique to
suggest that it is difficult to establish that teachers act on cultural differences
between themselves (as White) and their ethnic minority pupils. However,
these criticisms fail to acknowledge that varying types of resistance and
contestation which occur in schools relate quite clearly to the racialized,
gendered and class-specific backgrounds of the pupils exhibiting them. As
will be shown in the accounts of the young people interviewed in the study
and presented below, resistances were often located in pupils' wider
racialized and gendered positions. Forms of speech, dress and ways of
walking are often indicative of displaced contestations or resistances
(Aggleton 1987) and these expressions hold greater cultural currency when
used in an area (school) where Black pupils are in a numerical and power-
related minority.

Resistance, Contestation or Challenge?

Though it remains important for a study of pupils' schooling experiences to
explore whether they respond in resistant ways, there are certain issues
which must be addressed in order to theorize these responses effectively.
Resistance theorists have been criticized for 'launching too readily into
optimism without sufficiently articulating the constraints which limit and
subvert the transformative potential of resistance' (Sultana 1989: 289). The
debate is ongoing as to whether or not resistance to schooling embedded
within anti-school attitudes can actually effect change. However, if indeed
pupils do resist the practice of knowledge production which takes place in

schools, particularly where they feel this knowledge does not reflect them culturally or experientially, the transformative nature of their resistance is problematized when they cut themselves off from gaining any form of knowledge. In Sewell's (1997) study of the 'conformists' and 'rebels', he suggests that though in some cases pupils may reject the function of schooling and the attendant knowledge which schools offer them, they do not reject the power of knowledge. For some African-Caribbean pupils, knowledge is sought from Black communities, as they may feel that it is only within this sphere that they are adequately culturally and experientially reflected. They thus feel culturally distant from school. Sewell suggests therefore that these pupils believe:

> knowledge can be used for collective action and the eventual betterment of the condition of Black people. It is proof that students in this category do not close off the possibility of pursuing an emancipatory relationship between knowledge and dissent.
>
> (Sewell 1997: 119)

Therefore knowledge can encourage emancipatory dissent. However, Sewell suggests that the 'hedonists' who, like Willis's lads, rejected all forms of mental labour, have cut themselves off from the emancipatory possibilities which arise out of gaining forms of knowledge. In this way, rejecting the pursuit of all forms of self-knowledge (both within and outside of school), limits transformative possibilities. It thus becomes difficult to theorize the behaviours and attitudes of these pupils as 'resistant'. It is therefore important to acknowledge that the responses of all children to schooling are multiple and that not all oppositionality can be theorized as resistant. It is also important to identify what it is that is being resisted. However, this is not to suggest that the behaviours of Sewell's (1997) 'hedonists' were simply reactionary, as their responses to schooling did not exist in isolation of others' responses to them.

The work of Aggleton (1987) has been important in differentiating between intent and outcome in relation to pupil responses to schooling. This might suggest that rather than viewing the behaviours of Willis's 'lads' (and hence also the 'hedonists' in Sewell's study) as indicative of a rejection of 'mental labour', instead the young males were challenging principles of control within the school (Aggleton 1987: 128). Aggleton argues that it is necessary to differentiate between challenges against wider societal power relations and more localized principles of control, such as those occurring within schools. In this way it is possible to identify behaviours as resistant or contestual. Additionally, in differentiating between intent and outcome it becomes possible to view the contestations of Black pupils against specific processes within schools as having more resistant outcomes, in that often their responses are located within wider racialized discourses. Clearly, the added focus on school exclusion, and the power embedded within it as one of an educational institution's most important sanctions, will provide an additional emphasis on the nature of the power struggle between pupils and teachers within schools. With these theoretical considerations in mind, it is now possible to explore the resistant possibilities within pupil responses to schooling.

The Effect of Sanctions on Teacher–pupil Relationships

An important aspect of the experience of school sanctions, and one which is important to an analysis of pupil resistance and contestation, relates to the issue of power. Within the school environment relationships between pupils and teachers are structured on a basis of power and powerlessness. Resistance theories have often been criticized for assuming these relationships are unidirectional through placing students and teachers within predictable power positions (Mac an Ghaill 1995). The following accounts will show that pupils use forms of resistance/contestation to negotiate the form that their relationship with teachers will take. Much resistance was used to subvert the traditional teacher as powerful, student as powerless relationship. However, the power which teachers have to impose various school sanctions on pupils, culminating in school exclusion, adds a further dimension to the pupils' resistance. Contrary to the teacher's perceptions, these pupils did not exhibit anti-education sentiments. Rather, the pupils' responses were situated in their wider racial and gendered positions. Additionally, in similar ways to the 'macho lads' in Mac an Ghaill's (1995) study, the pupils' resistance was a response to the 'domination, alienation and infantilism' (1995: 57) they experienced. This was not always as a result of being situated in lower sets, as Mac an Ghaill suggests of his respondents, but in relation to the threat of school sanction and permanent exclusion which, under present education policy conditions, is continuously reinforced in schools (Blyth and Milner 1996).

The extent to which the responses of some pupils to school could be read as resistant was quite school-context dependent. Thus the school ethos discussed in the previous chapter and the extent to which particular pupils felt that they had a stake in it, depended on the use of school sanctions/ exclusions, the place of rewards within pastoral policy and the explanations drawn on by staff to account for pupil behaviour. In School D for example, many pupils interviewed had either experienced particular traumas outside school, including assault, discord between parents and partners and degrees of family poverty, or had developed particular roles within their local communities which were played out within their school peer groups. Others had learning difficulties which they attempted to mask in particular behavioural forms, the majority of which were conflictual. These circumstances were not 'race' specific. In a large number of cases where pupils were seen by staff to be behaving inappropriately, explanations were drawn from pupil circumstance. However, in other schools the extent to which staff would draw on alternative explanations for pupil behaviour did not often help to mediate in situations of conflict. In School A, the focus on academic standards meant that often despite other factors which may have also been contributing, badly behaved pupils were seen simply as badly behaved. In Schools B and E, where many pupils also experienced various social problems outside the school environment, both schools responded with numerous exclusions and other sanctions. In School B this left very little room for staff to draw on whatever background information might have been available about the child. Similarly, in School E sanctions were increasingly used because it was felt that many parents had either lost or abdicated responsibility for the control of their children.

In respect of this, the pupils who had experienced school exclusion in School D did not talk in terms of *resisting* particular aspects of school. There was much low level disruption present in many of the lessons observed and teachers readily pointed to the persistently difficult pupils in the school. On their part, pupils talked about not liking particular lessons teachers and some of the older pupils spoke of school as though it were an irritating interruption to their lives in their communities. The Head also commented that though many pupils caused disruption in classrooms, at a recent school inspection all pupils had been well behaved including those who were persistently disruptive. She commented that pupils had been *intentionally* punctual and attentive for the inspectors illustrating a degree of loyalty to the school which many of the staff had found pleasantly surprising. Therefore, rather than finding many pupils who wished to react against the control of their teachers at this school, there were instead groups of teachers, including those in senior positions reacting against the powerless positions they had been placed in both professionally and in terms of the poor reputation the school had developed over the years. This provides an interesting point of departure for theorizing resistance in schools and will be explored later in this chapter.

However it is necessary at the outset to note that pupil resistance must always be viewed in relation to what, if any, effects it can have on the position of the pupil. Although pupils may complain of differential treatment, the unfairness of particular policies or their inability to be heard by staff, it is the extent to which pupils respond, either verbally or behaviourally, to these circumstances that can lead to a discussion as to whether or not such resistances exist.

There have been instances where pupils have spoken of particular circumstances which they, and staff in their school pastoral team, have felt contributed to their experience of school sanctions. The forms of resistance displayed by pupils in school are not always simply an outcome of difficulties experienced within the school environment but problems they encounter outside school, for example, at home. However, traditional theorists have tended to focus mainly on the school (Willis 1977) but there have been situations where the two means of resisting have occurred.

In School B, as will be highlighted in Chapter 4, a number of pupils interviewed had gradually become aware of the changing focus on discipline. Mr Mills, the Headteacher, had made announcements in assemblies, in the school magazine and to the governors, about the changing discipline policy. Shahid, a Pakistani pupil in Year 10 commented on the changing policy in view of the restrictions it would place on him academically. He had a wide network of older friends outside school, and felt that should he not achieve well, he would become drawn into criminal activity.

> Since Mr Mills came back if a teacher says something to you and you don't even answer back, you just talk to them, they think you're answering back and then they go and tell Mr Mills and Mr Mills will exclude you like that. That's what's bad about him. He's too strict. I want to get my marks and get out of this school one time. When I get them now I'll [probably] end up in a hotel washing dishes. Because that's what you have to do nowadays. Cabbying, drug dealing. There is money in them things. Drug dealing, there's a lot of money in that. [But] the risk of getting caught, that's your life. Your life's unbearable. I'd rather be a normal guy that's got a job, who gets good pay.
>
> (Shahid, Pakistani pupil, Year 10, School B)

Shahid recognized that he had only a slim likelihood of achieving the examination grades that he needed in order to avoid the life led by many of his peer group in the local community, should he become caught up in the school's new 'fast track' to fixed-term exclusion. Some of the older friends in his peer group outside school had been excluded, and though he could see that exclusion was one of the most effective punishments that his school had available to it, its effectiveness was only short-lived.

Researcher: Which punishment do you think is the most useful punishment in the school?

Shahid: Exclusion [because] you can't come back.

Researcher: When you can't come back do you think this makes you change?

Shahid: No. You get involved in drug dealing and things like that. That's what most people do these days. They have no jobs, they spend their giros on drugs. I've grown up too quick and learnt too quick.

Unlike the rebels in Sewell's (1997) study of Black male resistance, Shahid does not place a greater value on the forms of knowledge gained within local communities than that gained in school. Shahid talks of the knowledge he has accrued about ways to be successful from spending time with his peers in his neighbourhood. But he does not want to be precipitated into this alternative means of achieving financial success through an experience of exclusion, and recognizes that the new policy in place at school may indeed put him in such a position. Shahid was involved in very low level classroom disruption, but only when a certain other pupil was present in his lessons. This pupil was often out of school on exclusions or spending time in the on-site unit and thus Shahid could avoid trouble. He had also experienced school sanctions for smoking, but did not pose a serious threat to the overall order of the school. However, the new discipline policy could make a potential casualty of a pupil such as Shahid and it is within this context that Shahid spoke about the inevitability of his educational career. Even with qualifications, he jokes that he may only achieve the status of washing dishes in hotels. Shahid therefore did not rebel against the function of education, but did have particular problems relating to Mr Mills the Headteacher. The extent of Shahid's resistance to Mr Mills was as low level in nature as his disruption and lay somewhat in the shadows of the responses of some of his African-Caribbean male peers. As he commented, in the light of the changing climate around discipline that the Headteacher had fostered:

Shahid: They [African-Caribbean Year 11 boys] all wear hats. You know when Mr Mills sees them he says 'yeah take your hat off'. Like me for example, if I'm wearing a hat if he sees me, he's like take it off there and then. But most of the time they argue back with him.

Researcher: But he's not scared of you seeing as he's always telling you to take off your hat?

Shahid: I'm not worried about him, I won't say nothing to that teacher. But if he done something serious to me, I'd wait for him outside the school premises. He would never ever walk in them areas especially in [his local area]. I'm not really scared to walk into anywhere, because I've got enemies and I can walk into their areas. If you get beat up, you get beat up. But him now, he's a bad teacher, I don't think anyone would let him walk into their area. All the people he's been bad to.

Shahid spoke almost as if he was in awe of the way that Nehemiah and many of the older African-Caribbean pupils in his school-based peer group (two of whom had since been excluded) had responded to Mr Mills. Theirs was a level of resistance which challenged the authority of Mr Mills to remove simple items of clothing from them. Such low level examples of indiscipline were clearly very difficult for Mr Mills to react against through the use of sanctions, although it was not impossible for him to do so. Rather, there was a certain fear of some of the older African-Caribbean boys that Shahid was certainly aware of and which appeared to prevent Mr Mills from using his authority in those immediate circumstances. Instead he was more likely to rely on the fast track procedure which would no doubt bring Nehemiah and his friends to his office, where he could issue them with an exclusion in relative safety.

Alternatively, Shahid spoke of the possibility of using a response against Mr Mills which would be vengeful, but was also highly unlikely. Rather Shahid viewed these interactions with Mr Mills as almost harmless, pointing out that he would respond to more serious concerns should they arise. Shahid's level of resistance was that he intended fully to remain within the school and achieve the qualifications that he needed in order to to avoid the otherwise inevitability of criminal behaviour that he spoke of. Thus he did not directly challenge Mr Mills on the occasions when he was asked to remove his hat. This in itself is not low level, but a quite well-developed way of resisting the threat of school exclusion. It is similar to the strategies adopted by the young Black female pupils in the work of Mirza (1992), Fuller (1982) and Mac an Ghaill (1988), who, whilst accepting the functions of schooling and the necessity of achieving well within it, rejected the institutions within which their education took place. The recognition of the importance of the value placed on education effecting a form of resistance has been questioned (Foster et al. 1996). However, Shahid continued to experience some difficulty at school and his avoidance strategies were not always successful.

Shahid presents an example of a pupil aware of what he needed to do in order to resist what he saw as Mr Mills' intentional attempts to remove him from the school. He was part of a peer group of boys who were seen as the serious disrupters to the order of the school and thus could derive a certain sense of safety from his position within this group. He was also aware of the wider issues at stake should he not succeed in his attempt at resistance. But whereas the activities of some of his peers acted as forms of resisting the authority of the new discipline policy, when Shahid took part in them it meant that his own resistant activity, achieving the grades necessary to leave school and do well outside was not being nurtured. It is also possible that such a long-term goal – Shahid was in Year 10 at the time of interview – was not having immediate effects for Shahid and its validity as a means of resisting the harshness of the new policy was limited.

Racializing Resistance

At School C, there was no similar ethos of harshness surrounding discipline as evident by the Head's views on the unhelpful concept of punishment (see Chapter 2). However, the legacy of the school's earlier approaches to school exclusion remained and some of the young people in Years 9–11 had known of pupils who had been excluded or asked to leave by senior members of staff. There were therefore similarities with School B in that both approaches to discipline – the about-turn in place at School C, and the new harsher regime at School B – had been seen as racialized by some of the young people who had become caught up in them. This second exploration of resistance draws upon the work of 'race' and education theorists (Gillborn 1990; Mac an Ghaill 1988; Wright 1985, 1987; Sewell

1997) in looking at young Black pupil definitions of teacher racism and their resistance to it.

School C had developed a complex pastoral system which involved the Deputy Head, two senior teachers responsible for pastoral issues across the school, a specific room in which these teachers were housed, followed by the hierarchies of Heads of Year, Heads of Departments and form tutors. The Headteacher, as with School A, did not have to necessarily become involved in disciplinary matters but would do so occasionally. One African-Caribbean Year 9 pupil was quite certain that the Deputy Headteacher, Ms Gotham, awarded sanctions differentially between Black and White students. She based this not only on her own experience of the teacher, but also on that of older pupils who had friends excluded by her in the past.

> 'Some of the teachers are racist. They've got favouritism. I don't get on with [Ms Gotham] because, well me personally, she's always picking on Black people. I'm not the only one that has said that. Even students in the upper years if you ask them. I know a couple of people in Year 10 and 11 and we asked them because we thought it was just us saying that. We asked them and they said, she is always picking on us as well.'
>
> (Nicola, African-Caribbean pupil, Year 9, School C)

Nicola qualifies her perception of the racism of Ms Gotham by commenting that 'she's always trying to think of a way to get to us lot'. She notes that when being told off by other teachers for what she recognizes as 'messing about' on the stairs and corridors, that Ms Gotham will always appear to transform low level childish behaviour into an activity which warrants more serious sanction.

> 'One day in assembly someone had let off some gas and me and my friends, we always sit together and we was all moving up. Ms Gotham asked to see us all after assembly and she said 'I'm keeping my eye on you lot because in lessons you are always getting in trouble'. But when we ask our teachers if we are all right, they say 'yes'. We don't understand why she is always saying that.'
>
> (Nicola, African-Caribbean pupil, Year 9, School C)

Nicola felt that she got on very well with all of her teachers apart from Ms Gotham and another female teacher. However, she was reacting to a situation which she felt was based on differentiation along racial lines. Nicola was involved in an educational programme set up in the school by a local Black voluntary organization and was achieving well through her involvement in the sessions. One of the two pastoral managers working under Ms Gotham, did not feel that this educational programme was particularly helpful to the pupils, as she felt that it attempted to change the way pupils responded to

White teachers in particular. The co-ordinator of the programme had helped some of the children to reflect before challenging teachers when they felt decisions made were wrong and the pastoral managers had become aware of this. Rather than valuing the changes, they were seen as particularly false and as contributing to a climate of racial tension.

Like Shahid above, Nicola did not take part in serious disruptive activities. She had experienced a fixed-term exclusion for hitting a girl who had barged into her after she had experienced an accident. She had recognized that she had been wrong and her parents had also been disappointed in her, but she felt that for some reason Ms Gotham simply did not *like* her and that she made a point of finding out whether or not Nicola had been in any trouble at the classroom level.

> 'Since I've come to this school, she's never liked me or my friends. My mum wanted to move me out of the school. I didn't want to leave because I'd made all my friends. [The first time] we was in the canteen and my friend Shanelle nicked some grits from the canteen. And [Ms Gotham] wanted, oh she really wanted me to be in it and I didn't do anything. And [Ms Gotham] went "oh did you do anything?" Shanelle said "no it was just me on my own". I thought why couldn't she just accept that. But she wants it to be me really badly so I get into trouble. The other day I found out this boy had a fight with another Year 10. They were investigating because they wanted to get to the bottom of it. I was at a funeral and my friend Shanelle got pulled out of a lesson by Ms Gotham. And [Ms Gotham] said "where's Nicola?" Shanelle said "she's gone to a funeral". [Ms Gotham] said "you know what I want to talk to you about, it's about the fight". She said "if anyone asks you, just say we are speaking about Nicola". Why does she have to use my name? Couldn't she use anyone else's name?'
>
> (Nicola, African-Caribbean pupil, Year 9, School C)

Nicola therefore is rejecting a form of teacher dislike. She is aware that she, and many of her friends, are being sought out by a particular teacher. She also recognizes that even in her absence she is being associated with, and in a sense implicated in, a negative incident, simply because she knows what may have happened. Though there is no immediate threat of school exclusion here, none the less, Nicola is aware from her conversations with other pupils that Ms Gotham seeks out particular groups of young people for her attention. It is the approach taken by Ms Gotham, trying to ensure that there is very little chance for Nicola to misbehave and Nicola's attendant perception that Ms Gotham does not like her as an individual, that is causing Nicola the most trouble. Nicola responds to Ms Gotham in a similar way to Shahid, above:

> 'My mum just said "ignore her". I can do it because I can stare Ms Gotham out. Like she will look at all my friends in assembly and they

will all just look back at her. Just look at her. Me, I'm not making her ruin my chances of being what I want to be in life. I will just stick it out because I haven't got that long left in school.'

(Nicola, African-Caribbean pupil, Year 9, School C)

Like the young Black women who 'resist within accommodation' (Mirza 1992; Fuller 1982), Nicola feels the best way to outwit and hence show a greater resistance to Ms Gotham is to achieve longer term educational goals. Nicola commented that she would like to go to university and recognizes what she would need to achieve in order to do so. However, Nicola also adopts shorter term coping strategies, which she perceives to be resistant to teachers who respond to her in ways which are similar to that of Ms Gotham.

Researcher: When you don't think you are in the wrong do you ever say something?

Nicola: I just leave it really. Because some of the teachers do lie a lot. My mum had to come in once. One day we had a Mr Cook I think his name was – my German teacher was away and he didn't know a German word because he teaches Russian. And he said 'does anyone know what [this] means? I said 'it's best to look it up in the dictionary'. He told me to get outside. Then he said get back in and I'll see you in my office. So I went and he said 'do you feel you were in the wrong?' I said 'no not really. I only said look in the dictionary because I thought that is what people do when you don't know a word.' He said he wanted to see my parents. He told my mum it was the attitude, the voice I said it in. After all that he looked it up in the dictionary anyway.

Researcher: What did your mum say?

Nicola: Mum said 'what's the point if you looked it up in the dictionary?' He said it was my attitude

Researcher: Do you think you speak to people in a certain tone of voice?

Nicola: If I'm in an angry mood I will. But the majority of the time, if I like the teachers and I get on with them I speak to them how I speak to my mum. I speak to them with respect. If I know the teachers don't like me, and I don't like them if they treat me badly, I will have a bad attitude towards them.

Mr Cook was one of the school-wide senior pastoral teachers who worked with Ms Gotham. Nicola was aware, as were the majority of pupils in the research, of the staff room gossiping which took place and felt that Mr Cook did not 'like her' in view of what he knew of her from Ms Gotham. Though she says that she will avoid responding to certain situations with teachers, which she clearly sees as forms of provocation, her use of 'attitude' in the interaction above was resistant. Nicola's resistance to the way she felt she had been 'picked on', in a process which appeared both lengthy and systematic, had built up since her arrival at the School in Year 7. What also had led to the build up of her resistance to senior members of staff was her inability initially to explain why she was experiencing difficulty with a particular teacher, and then her growing perception that she was simply not liked by certain members of staff. Although Nicola may appear as though she has made a final stand of defiance in front of Mr Cook, the feelings of rejection emerging from her constant negative interactions with Ms Gotham dictated her desire to avoid confrontation and simply ignore the teacher where possible.

The fraught relationship which existed between Nicola and Ms Gotham is situated within a climate towards discipline which was changing within the school. As mentioned in the previous chapter, the school was moving away from the image it had gained of being a high excluder of Black pupils. The Head had introduced new forms of classroom management for teachers, and they had been involved in much in-service training. However, the relationship of the staff to their Black pupils remained ambivalent, and Nicola's situation becomes quite interesting within this context. Though many teachers avoided talking directly about the racial differences of the pupils, they clearly perceived certain differences to exist between pupils. The new approach to discipline was balanced on the side of leniency, particularly for some of the pupils who may have required some work from pastoral staff. However, teachers in other schools had commented that the pastoral structure at School C was undeveloped, that the staff had received little training in defusing situations and that those defusing were more comfortable with confrontational approaches. Regardless of this the exclusion figures were gradually reducing, helped as pointed out by Nicola above, by some parents who were asked to withdraw their children, or indeed by others who *made the decision to withdraw themselves*. The circumstances under which these decisions were made varied, for example as with Nicola's mother, who was aware of the negative relationship developing between Ms Gotham and her daughter.

The Shape of Racism within Schools

Rather than introducing a climate in which Black pupils were increasingly sought out, as Nicola felt, one African teacher thought that the teachers were damaging the educational chances of Black children first by being too lenient with them, and then by resorting to exclusion once their behaviour had grown out of control.

'[Black children] live in a society where people just think if they say something they will be accused of racism. So they allow this to wear away. Children are not being dealt with at the initial stage. You don't allow it to get to that instance before dealing with it. People don't speak to most of the minorities because they are afraid to because of racism.

Personally I believe the teachers are not doing their job. I see my black students roaming about and nobody says anything to them. We know there's racism but they shouldn't use it as an excuse of doing nothing.'

(Mr Ogbu, Teacher, School C)

Mr Ogbu is speaking about those pupils who are left to their own devices until it becomes possible to exclude them permanently and thus is talking about a different group of Black pupils. However, this contrasts with the experience of Nicola and her group of Black female friends. She does not fit into the category of the pupils left alone by staff. Perhaps her involvement in the educational programme supported by the Black voluntary organization sets her apart from the pupils that Mr Ogbu despairs of. There may indeed be a multitude of other explanations, but it is clear that Nicola has sought a more immediate strategy to her schooling experience. Both of her strategies must, however, be situated within the climate of racialization which exists within her school.

However, Mr Ogbu makes an important point surrounding the responses of staff to ethnic minority pupils, which he perceives to be one of initial avoidance with almost intentional outcomes, and Nicola sees as one of confrontation and differentiation. Pupils who responded to the existence of racism in their interactions with staff did so because of a real perception of differential treatment. All of the young women in Nicola's 'gang' were of African-Caribbean and mixed parentage. The group of young men who Mr Mills wanted to 'weed out' of his school described earlier by Shahid, were African-Caribbean and, as will be highlighted in the chapter to follow, many other pupils at this school felt differential experiences of school sanction existed between Black and White pupils. There were occasions, however, which Mr Ogbu may be alluding to, where racism was seen by pupils who would then admit later on that it had not actually existed. However, this behaviour was rare among the pupils. It was often the case that they would interpret particular responses of staff as racist or believe certain comments to be racist. Even where in some cases it was doubtful that a racist incident had taken place, what is important is that the pupils' experience of that incident was that it *had* been racist and that it was a real perception.

'I do think sometimes, this might sound awful, it might come out wrongly, but sometimes they can use racism to exclude their behaviour. Their behaviour, if it's wrong doesn't matter what race you are it's still wrong. It's got to be dealt with.'

(Mrs Frank, Head of Year 10, School A)

Mrs Frank is of course quite correct that where behaviour has been wrong it should be treated as such and that teachers should respond to all indications of misbehaviour equitably. However, many pupils saw that others were being allowed to continue misbehaviour whilst they would receive a sanction. Where the pupils allowed to continue misbehaving were White, ethnic minority pupils came to what they saw as a logical conclusion, thus placing all of their strategies to resist the authority of that teacher within a racial context.

> 'You get different kinds of racism, you get undercover racism as well. They react in different ways, treat us different from Whites.'
> (Chantel, mixed parentage, Year 10 pupil, School B)

As with research conducted by theorists exploring Black pupil experiences of school (Gillborn 1990), White pupils were also aware of differentials.

> 'Someone told the teacher what was going on. I was about to light up and Miss Brown walked in. [The others] weren't smoking, they were just hanging around. [Miss Brown] said to my mum 'Chantel was there so she must have been smoking too'. Chantel went mad. [And] Mr Mills, he's a racist and he knows that. I had my nose pierced and Donna got hers done. He didn't say anything to me but because they've got theirs done now, he's always telling them off. Now that doesn't mean he's racist but I know that he is. Everyone knows. He's always picking on Black people.'
> (Lisa, White Year 9 pupil, School B)

Thus differential experiences of school sanction and teacher attention were qualified by pupils as indicative of racism, although in Lisa's account above, she seems unsure of what racism might mean. Racism itself, though underplayed by some teachers initially created a context where much misunderstanding and conflict took place. However, pupils felt that some teachers failed to respond adequately to their concerns, whereas for some others they were able to seek sanctuary with particular teachers whom they felt would listen and take complaints on board. Each school had developed equal opportunities policies and whereas in School D, this and the anti-racist philosophy of the school was discussed with all pupils by all teachers when they arrived in Year 7, in School C for example, Black professionals were brought in to add the necessary 'multicultural' focus to the school. Gillborn (1990) warns against developing anti-racist policies which are 'merely an empty exercise by which yet another document is produced to be debated, adopted and ultimately forgotten by the majority of teachers' (Gillborn 1990: 119). In the majority of schools equal opportunities statements prohibited racial harassment and name calling among peers in school. Very rarely do such documents look at the possibility of racism occurring between staff and pupils where staff, rather than pupils are the perpetrators. Within this context therefore, staff were not willing to accept the accusations of racism levelled by some of the pupils above, and were more inclined to see them as excuse making, or simply malicious.

'He thinks that everything that anybody ever tells him off for is to do with the colour of his skin. He doesn't think that it's to do with his behaviour. It's like some women think that everything that goes wrong in their life is because they are a woman. Whereas it might be because of their personality. I don't get promotion because I'm a woman. In fact they don't get promotion because they are not good enough. I wish I felt happier to deal with it. But I'm concerned that if I once go down that road, I might get labelled as being racist.'

(Mrs Keys, Assistant Head of Department, School B)

Mrs Keys sees herself as a victim of her attempts to challenge what a particular pupil has said. Teachers are seen as non-racist individuals because of their status within the school and the likelihood that a child has used the accusation in order to get him/herself away from a troubled situation (Gillborn 1990). For other Black members of staff however, the experience of being seen as racist by Black pupils was particularly worrying.

'Worst I've ever been called was by an Afro-Caribbean kid that had been excluded. It was about coconuts. I found that in many ways quite wounding, insulting. It wasn't because it was from another Black person to another Black person. But by the nature of it. You condemn [their] behaviour and that therefore somehow you are negating the colour of your skin you know. I find that quite offensive. Apart from the fact when he first said anything I couldn't understand what it was I asked somebody and I think one of the parents told me. You know black on the outside, white on the inside. I hadn't got a clue.'

(Mr Cheatle, Deputy Head, School A)

The Deputy Head suggests that he was not hurt by the name given to him by the pupils because of the pupil's racial background. However, it is clear that this has had some impact on him particularly in the racialized context developing within the school which will be explored in Chapter 4.

Understandings of racism for Black staff were quite similar to those expressed by pupils. In School C where the issue of school exclusion had become increasingly racialized, the focus on Black children in staff discussions was worrying.

'I think every school has [racism]. I think there is racism at School B. Whenever I'm sitting in the staffroom, sometimes you'll be sitting in the[re] and you'll hear the staff going on about this list of kids. And 8 times out of 10 it will be a list of Black kids. No I'm not saying ... some of them are bad. Nehemiah, he's just completely barmy, and the only way to cope with Nehemiah is to laugh at him and laugh with him. Once you start being heavy, you get into a confrontation situation and you've lost it. I feel sad that [another African-Caribbean boy] was permanently excluded, he's another statistic. You've got to learn how to survive in the system. You know you see so many of them [Black pupils] wearing the headphones and big baggy coats. And I think "I know what my view of you is but what are White teachers' views of these Black pupils?". And you can't get an honest answer to that because if you ask white teachers they will say "I've got no problems with Black pupils, I treat everyone the same". This is the standard answer. So you can't really get to the root of it and the causes of the problem. Some of the teachers cannot cope with the Black kids, just in terms of talking to them. And that's where the problems stem from, if they could talk to them in a different manner.'

(Mr Shotter, Subject teacher, School B)

However, he felt that pupils talking about racism among staff was not the way to move beyond the potential of becoming another statistic. He did feel that racism was present, but he felt it essential for Black pupils to use responses more effectively to achieve change, rather than simply reacting to what they perceived to be racist comments.

Teacher Understandings of Resistance

The case studies presented above are only a few of the indications of pupils' resistance to various forms of authority from among those interviewed. Pupils resisted in a variety of other ways to their schools. Other pupils in School B, who were disappointed with the buildings in which the majority of their learning took place, developed a lack of respect for them. Litter was found everywhere, and some children had even begun to spit in corridors. The only places in the school where carpet could be found were the offices of senior teachers. The staff room was also not carpeted, which many of the pupils did not actually know, but would not have disrupted their means of rejecting the conditions in which they were expected to work. The rules which had been promoted in the school at the beginning of the year in tandem with the new discipline policy were rejected by many pupils, primarily because they felt they had not had a say in their development.

'[School rules] are important but nobody does them. They put them how a teacher would look at it.'

(Chantel, mixed parentage, Year 10 pupil, School D)

Another pupil in School A, who felt alienated from the school ethos around high academic standards due to his learning difficulties, also disagreed with the rules at his school

'Nobody goes by them [rules]. When people ask us to do something, when someone puts a rule up saying don't do this, they [pupils] think

"I'll go against it". It's like everyone has got to prove something.'
(Richard, White Year 9 pupil, School A)

An Indian pupil at School C felt that the boundaries were constantly being changed by his teachers, which is reflective of the changing climate around discipline within which Nicola's experiences were situated.

'[You're] messing around with the teacher, the teacher laughs and then when you say something else and the teacher sends you out because they don't like what you're saying, I think "what did I do? You were laughing and I get sent out".'
(Deep, Indian, Year 10 pupil, School C)

Deep responded by verbally challenging his teachers when he felt that they were in the wrong. Many teachers comment on this behaviour by pupils which is seen as indicative of insolence. For the pupils, it is often the only opportunity they have to 'save face' when they have had a confrontation with a teacher which has taken them completely by surprise. Pupils require extraordinary levels of sophistication to be able to cope with individual teachers, particularly in view of the speed at which teachers can respond to them differently in a variety of different situations (Reid 1987). It is therefore necessary for teachers to engage in consistent behaviour wherever possible as pupils can be particularly sensitive to a teacher who laughs and jokes with them at one stage and then decides the jokes are no longer funny the next.

The extent to which a pupil's negative response to particular aspects of school are recognized by their teachers can illustrate whether or not that pupil's behaviour is resistant. The resistant activities of Black pupils who wear specific items of clothing, or use particular ways of responding to teachers that are culturally specific (i.e. kissing their teeth, talking to each other in patois), were not always interpreted by staff as forms of behaviour which meant anything other than insolence (Wright 1985; Gillborn 1990; Mac an Ghaill 1988). The extent to which these practices can therefore effect change for the pupils concerned is questionable (Sultana 1989), although the use of these practices as a means of regaining personal dignity and as a coping strategy cannot be disregarded (Gillborn 1990). However, in certain cases teachers are aware of the strategies used by pupils and of the reasons behind them and where pupils have been successful in transmitting their anger and frustrations to staff, the transformative possibilities of their contestual behaviours are increased. Thus for example, although it is unlikely that any member of staff at School C could prevent the disadvantage present in the community in which Shahid lived, introducing a more tolerant conception of discipline may have gone some way towards enabling him to remain in school and sit the examinations that would find him employment.

However, though teachers may recognize why pupils resist their control, unless they are in a position to assist them, the knowledge is of no use. One White male technology teacher in School C was the form tutor for an African-Caribbean girl who was badly behaved with almost all of her teachers. His comment, however, was that the majority of teenage girls are disaffected, and that there is very little a school can do to prevent that. Keys and Fernandes (1994) found that pupils' attitudes to school tend to deteriorate between the ages of 11 and 14 and it has been suggested that 'deviant behaviour is a normal part of growing up and a part of becoming a person in one's own right' (McManus 1989: 76). The behaviour of young people therefore can be unpredictable and the technology teacher has suggested an awareness and acceptance of his tutee's behaviour. However, in this respect, the tutor's response to the pupil's behaviour and the frustration with schooling that it demonstrates, will not enable that young woman to move beyond whatever has created her disaffection. School C, in moving from a fairly harsh response to the pupils on its roll it considered undesirable has adopted a *laissez-faire* approach to discipline. Whereas other schools with similar pupils may attempt to look at the reasons behind the behaviour of pupils and work with pupils to resolve difficulties as far as possible, the positive teaching approach adopted by staff at School C does not enable them to use their evaluations of pupils to any great effect.

Another teacher, at School B noticed that the children seemed more fatalistic in their attitudes towards education and their futures generally, than in any other school she had taught in. However, she identified that in many cases children were more restricted in School B.

'There is a very different attitude here from the pupils. I sense a lot more hopelessness here than I saw before. There seems to be a much more fatalistic attitude. [There is] much more aggression here against the school and authority in general than I have seen elsewhere. I mean the set-up, the rules, the expectations are no different from one place to another. Certainly most schools I have worked in there has been more pupil freedom. The school I came here from was similar to this but we had an open school policy where doors were left open all the time. Pupils had access all the time. But there was never any damage or vandalism. Whereas during my time here there have been experiments in doing that, but it has resulted in so much damage [so] the opportunity has been taken away.'

(Miss Bean, Head of Department, School B)

At School B there was a very clear division between senior management staff and the rest of the school and as Miss Bean has noted, there was not an open door policy currently in place. She also suggests that the open door policy was tried once but did not work. It is likely that children's perceptions of the huge distinctions between themselves and senior members of staff were well formed by the time the school decided to change to a more relaxed approach to teaching. In this climate therefore, no change would have been successful, and pupils interviewed commented on their opinion of the state of the school buildings and increasing antagonism between them and the senior staff who gave them sanctions for poor behaviour. However, in understanding the behaviour of the pupils who are disruptive in school, Miss Bean places the blame of the ills of her pupils at the door of society generally

> 'There are an awful lot of pupils we are seeing going through school who know, or who anticipate that they are never going to work. And therefore what is the point? We can't offer them that carrot any more of "work hard in school and you'll do OK", because some of them won't regardless of their ability in some cases. Society is shaped in such a way that we can no longer offer full-time employment to everybody. We haven't got to a stage where we can offer them an alternative. How many are going home seeing parents who don't work? Where there is no hope of work in communities, where a lot of people have no hope of work? 10 years ago you could say to a child, if you work hard at school this will happen. Although we may still say that, for an awful lot of people it's not true.'
>
> (Miss Bean, Head of Department, School B)

This teacher is aware of the difficulties which may inform the behaviour of some of the children in the school and many of her opinions were shared by other members of teaching staff at the school. There was an increasing level of cynicism by some of the non-senior teachers, which not only reflected the sense of hopelessness they felt for many of their pupils, but also the fact that particular processes within the school itself either aggravated or failed to respond to these pupil needs. As Docking (1987) suggests:

> '[T]he behaviour of any human being at any particular time is materially affected by the context in which she or he is placed ... The main factors which predispose many children to behave unacceptably may lie outside the immediate control of the school, but the extent to which a child realizes any tendency to behave badly will depend upon the quality of life experienced at school. Children who experience a high level of stress due to disharmony in the home, for instance, may or may not use the school to vent their frustration, depending upon their perception of what is expected of them at school and how they believe they are valued in the school community.'
>
> (Docking 1987: 16)

Understanding Racialized Resistances

Resistances against situations seen as unfair were not restricted to pupils in schools. Teachers, who feel powerless against policy changes made by senior members of staff, who are not consulted on major school decisions, who teach in schools which are seen as 'sin bins' and, most importantly for the issue under present discussion, reject the use of school exclusion, are likely to attempt to use their positions as teachers to assist their pupils as far as possible within these restricted contexts. Often teachers are presented as an undifferentiated category by pupils within schools, as indeed are pupils by their teachers. However, where particular school approaches to the issue of exclusion have not worked effectively, this is usually because they are resisted by both pupils and some members of staff. In addition to this, the fatalistic attitude to the situations of some pupils described above, will not be shared by all staff, and as one teacher pointed out in relation to the underachievement of Black male pupils 'you shouldn't just say look at this awful statistic, you say what can we do about it, who can we work with?'. It is unlikely that these members of staff can affect forms of resistance to particular school-based or wider educational policies. In the same way despite the resistance of many pupils to their negative relations with some staff, it was not enough to alter them. However, the contesting of unfair practices can challenge, however temporarily, the powerless position within which unhappy individuals have been placed.

When speaking of differentiating the category of teachers, an immediate starting point relates to that of 'race'. Though there were very few Black teachers in the schools visited, many of them saw their roles as teachers extending beyond the ordinary teacher–pupil relationship. Much work has pointed out the complex positions that Black teachers find themselves placed in (Callender 1998; Sewell 1997), particularly where they find themselves teaching in a minority, or in schools where Black children are experiencing educational problems.

The pupil population in School E was almost entirely made up of White children. There was one African-Caribbean female pupil in Year 9, and three mixed parentage pupils. Interestingly all were selected by senior staff as pupils who gave teachers cause for concern. Within this environment there were only two ethnic minority members of staff. One, an African-Caribbean male, was the site manager for the school and thus had no teaching responsibilities at all, and the other was an African-Caribbean science teacher.

'I think you have to establish yourself with the staff because I think when I first started teaching people were very suspicious, because I was the only Black teacher on the staff. Also the relationship with the kids can be a strain at times. I've had one incident of racial abuse, I've had two since I've been here, so I suppose that's not bad. They still have latent ideas about Black people, and it's not until you start talking to them, and they make an off-the-cuff remark, that you realize that it's just underneath the surface. A classic one was when they were collecting for charity, and one of the kids in my form said 'I hope it's not going to them Black people in Africa' So I said 'what's wrong with that?' He said 'we should be spending it here.'

(Mrs Lewis, Science Teacher, School E)

Unlike some of the other Black teachers interviewed who felt that they could support Black pupils or at least assist their colleagues when responding to ethnic minority pupils, Mrs Lewis felt that the Black pupils at School E were looked after by other pupils, despite the racial antagonism that existed in the local community.

'It's a particular syndrome that you find in certain football teams. If you're on this estate, if you've got ties on this estate, and you're a Black kid or a mixed race kid, you're going to be alright. If you're an incomer from another place, you won't be accepted and your experience here will be terrible. We've had examples of that where a family was moved in from somewhere but they had their house broken into, garage set alight and all sorts of atrocious things. The woman ended up having a stand up battle with another parent in the street and then it just went downhill from there. So if you've gone to one of the junior schools and you've come up through that system where you've known kids, and you've come here, that's OK. It's not very pleasant and there's quite a lot of racist attitudes to Asians. I know a lot of Asian kids go to School B rather than come here.'

(Mrs Lewis, Science Teacher, School E)

Other Black teachers were critical of their colleagues who refused to take racial differences of the pupils into account.

'In an inner city school I'm surprised by the lack of knowledge some of my colleagues have about others who come from Black African-Caribbean and Asian backgrounds. I think it's appalling. Your view is different and your perception of the world you live in is different. I think if you are a Black teacher and you have got some political awareness of the issues, then you bring those views to the school and you can see things in a way that I don't think White teachers ever see because I don't think they understand. I don't think White teachers understand contemporary Black youth culture, they don't understand how it affects young people. Some of the things that Black kids have said to teachers, I don't think they mean it in the way that the teachers have taken it. They're just rapping and the teachers say "who do you think you are talking to me like that?" When all they need to say is "yeah and you too".'

(Mr Shotter, African-Caribbean, Subject teacher, School B)

And in view of the difficulties colleagues may experience in understanding particular cultural aspects, Black teachers were faced with a lot of responsibilities both to their colleagues and to other Black pupils

'I think it's very lonely and very hard being a Black teacher which White teachers don't understand and don't appreciate because you work in a real sense of isolation. And you have to compromise yourself. Because you've got to fit into a White working environment. You can't say the things you want to say, you can't do the things you want to do because you've got to fit in with the context of the other people. Kids judge you straight away and they judge you as a Black teacher. It's even harder as a Black teacher because if I fail in my job, I'm letting down the Black kids in this school and further Black teachers. Whereas if I do a good job as Black teachers then firstly, hopefully I'll get the respect of the kids and secondly the respect of my fellow members of staff and thirdly any other Black teachers who apply for jobs here.'

(Mr Shotter, African-Caribbean Subject Teacher, School B)

Thus the cultural misunderstandings which arose between some of the Black pupils in School B and the White members of staff often escalated into conflict which Mr Shotter clearly felt was avoidable. However, although he had the knowledge which could assist some Black pupils in confrontations that may develop with staff, this teacher clearly could not always be available to interpret for his colleagues what particular pupils may have meant, or alternatively to prevent the type of responses Black pupils would give to staff whom they perceived to be crossing particular cultural boundaries. There were clearly some things that he as an African-Caribbean teacher could say to pupils, but which would not be received in a similar way if said by a teacher who did not share that cultural background. Mr Shotter felt that staff needed to come to their own understanding of cultural differences rather than rely on him.

Understanding why particular ethnic minority pupils were resistant to aspects of school was not welcomed as readily by all ethnic minority teachers. And whereas Mr Shotter would engage in specific forms of banter, which interestingly he could only do with the majority of the African-Caribbean *male* pupils that he taught, others felt that to do so would cross the professional, and power-related boundaries between themselves and pupils.

'When you're outside of school and they're Jamaican, they'll want to talk to you as if they're Jamaican. So it's the language that they come out with and they think because it's a Black teacher so therefore I will speak to them that way. If it's a White teacher then I will not, or I will and they will not understand it. I had some Year 9s in here yesterday and one of them started coming out with all this patois and I said "I beg your pardon?" And he was gesturing and all this. So I said to him, "can I have a word with you outside? I don't mind how you speak when you're outside of school, but I don't want this in here. Just because you see a Black teacher you think oh I can get away with it because it's a Black

member of staff''. And there was a lot of buts and buts but in the end I
think they realized what I was trying to say to them.'
>   (Ms Donald, African-Caribbean, Subject teacher, School D)

For this teacher there were specific situations when the sharing of a cultural
background in a way that was not accessible by other White members of
staff/pupils, was not acceptable. In an environment where Black teachers are
in more of a minority that the pupils themselves, it is often necessary for
professional boundaries to be maintained in order that respect be gained from
staff.

Others who did not feel particularly marginalized within their schools
were likely to approach the issue of 'race' more confidently with Black
pupils. Some felt it their duty to do so whereas others did not mind that
pupils from a similar background felt comfortable talking to them about
particular issues.

'There will be an extra sensitivity on my part to the progress and
behaviour of Asian and Afro-Caribbean people. I'm not stressing *better*.
I'm not saying its nice, I'm just saying there's an extra sensitivity there. I
can say things to both those groups that may be some of my White
colleagues would shy away from. I can more easily bring to the attention
of Afro-Caribbean and Asians, that I found it can sometimes be hard and
prejudiced and that having a good education is one of the ways in which
you can break down some of those barriers,'
>   (Mr Cheatle, African-Caribbean, Deputy Head, School A)

'There are some students who will say something in one of the
languages and try and be a bit more pally with me, asking me questions
about my background and I will answer it quite truthfully. I don't mind
at all. They'll ask me things like do you wear a sari? Or do you do this,
do you like Indian music. Well that's my culture so I'll say yes, no,
whatever. We relate more because they know they've got someone in a
position of authority who is one of them.'
>   (Miss Kular, Indian, Subject teacher, School C)

For another, trying to help Black children proved to be difficult, but he
still felt that helping them to succeed was important, regardless of their
opinion.

'The caring is different. You care more. The value is different. They
[Black pupils] can hate me provided I think I am doing the right thing.
You want them to like you when you are destroying them, then you are
not helping them. Because these are people who really need education in
order to go forward. They don't want to be told off, they don't want to be
corrected. If you allow them to do whatever they're doing they'll be

your best friend. Because you don't allow [it] they say who are you to challenge me when no other person challenges me?'

(Mr Ogbu, African, Subject teacher, School C)

Conclusion

There are clearly many instances where the behaviour/attitudes of individuals within schools may be read or interpreted as resistant. However, as has been suggested here, the possibilities of deeming behaviour resistant can rely on the extent to which such behaviour effects change for the resisting individual. The oppositional acts and attitudes highlighted within this chapter by Shahid, for example, demonstrated that there is not a simple relationship between opposition and resistance. Even where the use of 'attitude' by Nicola to respond to a classroom situation may have had more immediate resistant effects – her teacher Mr Cook eventually looked up the word he was unsure about in the dictionary and Nicola was thus briefly vindicated – the likelihood that her 'attitude' could solve longer term problems would be more difficult to achieve. Much pupil 'oppositionality' involves 'face-saving' where they have felt embarrassed by teacher action or the experience of sanction. But it is rare that such action can achieve the longer term objectives of theorized resistance. Rather it is important that an understanding of racialized pupil resistance within schools take into account that often resistant actions on the part of Black pupils are a response to a relationship with the school that has built up negatively over time. The outcome of the resistance is only ever temporal – Nehemiah and his friends can refuse to remove their hats for their Headteacher to the extent that he will move away from the situation and the relations of power are temporarily reversed until, of course, their actions result in exclusion or other sanction.

It is also important to look at the place of 'race' within the resistance debate. Actions, attitudes and other signifiers can become imbued with racial meaning, but this can be interpreted differently by the various parties involved in the education process. Teachers considered references to 'racism' which can be employed by some students as indicative of excuse, whereas pupils may read racism in teacher actions, and perceive teacher indifference to their concerns as further evidence that racism has taken place. It is important that discussions around racism be held openly, as it is at the basis of much Black pupil resistance within school. However, racism itself is also undercut by the gendered discourses which place Black boys and girls in different levels of conflict and hence varying rates of exclusion within schools. It is to these gendered discourses that we will now turn.

4 Interrelations of 'Race' and Gender in School

Introduction

The previous chapter detailed many of the processes through which ethnic minority pupils would attempt to resist alienating aspects of their schooling. However, in many ways the responses of pupils to the use of sanctions within schools is mediated through their racialized and gendered backgrounds. The similarities in the responses of Nicola and Shahid highlight previously illustrated particular desires to succeed despite the perceived attempts of staff to prevent their achievement. If we compare this with the responses of Shahid's African-Caribbean male friends to the threat of school sanction/ exclusion, it is clear that there are particular processes which work to increase the alienation experienced by Black male pupils, and so cement their presence in fixed-term and permanent exclusion statistics. It was also notable that many of the pupils referred to by the ethnic minority staff in the previous chapter, were also Black and male. Research has begun to detail the production of early masculinities through the exploration of male pupil responses to school (Connell 1989; Mac an Ghaill 1995) and school masculinities have also been linked with constructs of 'race' (Sewell 1997). These various pieces of research have provided important theoretical and empirical insights into the experiences of African-Caribbean and Asian male pupils. However, in neglecting aspects of the interrelation of 'race' and gender in Black pupil identities, some theorists have only been able to offer a partial view of racialized pupils' responses. The focus on 'race' and schooling, as with other research on Black sub-cultural forms, has too often concentrated on the experiences of Black males. Thus in a similar way to the processes through which many acts of indiscipline have become associated by teachers with Black male behaviour, current educational and sub-cultural research has begun to equate Black identities and forms of resistance with masculinity (Mama 1995; Weekes 1996).

The current focus on school exclusions and the disproportionate exclusions of African-Caribbean males has also created assumptions about the anti-school attitudes of Black male pupils. This entirely negates the important work which has shown Black pupils to have pro- as well as anti-school responses within education (Furlong 1985; Fuller 1982; Sewell 1997; Gillborn 1990). Clearly the experiences of Black pupils in school are mediated through their gendered identities, and the way masculinity is portrayed within schools can play a large part in the relationships that exist between Black males, their peers and teachers. Young males, regardless of racial background, experience disproportionate exclusions from school. The fact that young African-Caribbean males are up to six times more likely to be excluded than any other group (Osler 1997), indicates that their schooling experiences are mediated through more than simply masculinity. Any discussion around the education of African-Caribbean males in schools must not simply be reduced to that of 'gendered exclusivity'. Though we will build on the gradually increasing work on Black schooling masculinity (Mac an Ghaill 1994; Sewell 1997), we shall depart from it through arguing for a more thorough interrelating of the effects of 'race' and gender. We shall also suggest that it is important to move away from theorizing these masculinities as a form of 'machismo', which is quite clearly racialized, as to do so may only pathologize the very different ways that young Black males respond to their experiences in school.

Work is increasingly being conducted on Black masculinities in schooling. What is now needed is research that does not only interrogate the ways in which masculinity is theorized, but also needs to build on the work of Mirza (1992), Fuller (1982) and Riley (1985), in order to address how schools also produce Black femininities. Feminist work in this area has tended to subsume the construct of 'race' within that of gender (McRobbie 1978). This has implications for the study of young Black women in schools, in view of the influence of race on the way in which they are responded to. The experiences of Nicola in the previous chapter, illustrate how she felt her racial background to have influenced her relationship with her teacher. And it is clear that in exploring the ways that both African-Caribbean males and females respond to aspects of their education, it will be possible to explore how the wider processes which may lead to school exclusion are reflected in the greater presence of Black boys in exclusion statistics.

Additionally, Asian pupils often acknowledge the equating of African-Caribbean masculinity with disruption. They have also been shown to display identities which incorporate empathy for their peers (Mac an Ghaill 1988; Gillborn 1990). The exploring of 'race' and gender in pupil adaptations to schooling not only throws up issues around pupil resistance and the inability of teachers to recognize racial stereotyping in their interactions with some pupils. It also suggests that definitions of masculinity and femininity are *produced* within schools and this has implications for Black male and female pupils. As highlighted towards the end of the previous chapter, teachers clearly do not constitute a homogenous category. The way they adapt to their own positions as teachers can depend upon the relative power/powerlessness this may confer upon them in relation to the reputation of the schools they teach in, or indeed their identities as Black/

White female/male members of staff. Furthermore, their own racial and gendered positions can have a direct bearing on the way they interact with their pupils and it is within this context that masculinities and femininities are produced within the educational environment.

School-based Genders

Historically, feminist researchers on the reproduction of gender divisions within education have focused on the implicit and explicit forms of masculinity which exist within schools (Davies 1984). This aspect of researching gender focused more on the need to integrate girls into technical and science subjects, than on the way boys took up masculine identities (Connell 1989). However, feminist research in this area did reveal an ethos within education which promoted qualities of individualism, competitiveness and differentiation, and this ethos has been theorized as masculine (Askew and Ross 1988). If young females are conceptualized as oriented towards personal relationships and males towards structures and role differentiation, then the basic principles of education within schools are at odds with the social orientation of girls and favour the ways that boys in general are socialized. Additionally, the processes by which achievement is measured through the comparison of one child with another, fosters forms of competitiveness, often aggressive, which coincide not only with young male social orientation, but also the 'technical-limited rationality' seen to dominate the marketplace (Ohrn 1993; 148). However, the important work of feminist researchers in education has highlighted, and in many ways helped to address, the educational performances of young women in schools, e.g. the documented increasing educational achievements of girls in comparison to boys can be seen as evidence of this, particularly in the case of African-Caribbean young women (Gillborn and Gipps 1996).[1]

Given the findings of research which point to the increasing exclusion of boys from both primary and secondary schools (Parsons 1996), work on schooling masculinities has attempted to explore how schools contribute to the formation of different male identities (Connell 1989; Mac an Ghaill 1994). The various masculine identities which schools construct are not all valued on a similar scale. For example, it has been suggested that the masculinities which are approved and legitimated within the educational sphere provide access to higher education and the professionals. Not all boys are given equal access to this provision and the masculine identity it affords. Definitions of masculinity within education then, are based upon binary oppositions of success/failure which are both class and race specific. It is the male identities of young working-class and Black males which come into conflict with those of White male teaching staff, and young middle-class male pupils (Mac an Ghaill 1994).

Recent policy changes within education which focus on competition between schools, the high status national curriculum and the introduction of 'hard, lean' market forces (Metcalf and Humphries 1985: 11) have been described as the New Right's attempt to 'remasculinize' the teaching profession and the education system (Mac an Ghaill 1994). Working-class and Black male pupils fall foul of these dominant definitions of schooling masculinity through being responded to as academic failures. They then take up different expressions of masculinity in order to find other forms of power which may include 'sporting prowess, physical aggression, sexual conquest' (Connell 1989: 292). The current Labour government's increased drive on school standards will do little to change the way that education has become associated with aggressive forms of competition. However, the introduction of 'softer' elements such as the drive towards improving literacy for all pupils, the increased push for the reduction of school exclusions and indeed the publication of school exclusion statistics, combines with legacies of the Conservative government to produce similar casualties. Schools are still expected to produce the highest achievers and in order to do so, and to compare effectively in the drive for standards, particular groups will continue to be discarded. Hence, the 'back door' exclusions, such as those used by senior teachers in School C are likely to become more popular and extensive.

The area of school sanctions and exclusions throws up particular tensions around power and powerlessness as between teachers and pupils. Mac an Ghaill (1994) suggests that though the male identities of young white working-class and Black boys are not seen to be as legitimate as others within schools, they remain more powerful than the identities of females. However, the extent to which African-Caribbean males are excluded from schools over and above their female peers, illustrates that any power Black males may experience by virtue of their gendered backgrounds can only ever be temporary. The gendered responses of the ethnic minority pupils interviewed to the threat of school exclusion and teacher sanction are situated within this context. Masculinity and femininity will not be the only mode through which these pupils will respond to school exclusion, 'race' also acts as a marker for these school-produced genders and the extent of this will be explored below.

Racializing Exclusion in the Image of Males

By virtue of the over-representation of Black young men in exclusion statistics, concepts of disruption and disaffection have at their centre the image of Black male subjects. Within four out of the five case study schools, Black boys had received the majority of school exclusions. School E, which had a very small number of ethnic minority students, had higher exclusions of White boys. The previous chapter illustrated the processes leading to school exclusion which were mediated through various forms of pupil and teacher resistance. Here the processes leading to exclusion were underpinned by responses to a variety of definitions of masculinity. The fact that school exclusion had become heavily racialized within a number of schools through the numbers of Black young people, and males especially, experiencing the sanction, also raised issues around the way that notions of 'race' were understood.

One such example of the association of exclusion with particular notions of 'race' was found within School B. Here the occurrence of fixed-period exclusions involved increasing numbers of Black pupils, and although the general issue of exclusions was discussed in non-racial terms the representation of particular groups of pupils within the school's statistics clearly had racialized implications. Prior to the research, the Headteacher had conducted a study to explore whether or not the experiences of Black pupils in the school was a result of racism. He concluded that it was not and that many of the Black male pupils in particular appeared to be more aggressive (and more likely to receive sanctions) than other pupils. He also related the maleness of the Black pupils, and the aggression they exhibited, to their female-headed, lone-parental backgrounds. It was within this context that the new discipline policy described in Chapter 2 took place with its consequence, an immediate rise in the exclusion of Black male pupils. Thus not only had the issue of school exclusion within this school become quite heavily racialized, but it was racialized in the image of the young Black male.

Chantel: Do you know how many Black pupils he's [the head teacher] excluded? Seventeen last time I looked. I was the first Black girl to be excluded. It was all boys and then we ... it was like we was putting up a stubborn way. If he spoke to us we would just walk off and kiss our teeth after him. He started excluding White people to style it out. He said 'we're going to kick all the clowns out...'

Researcher: How have you all reacted to that?

Chantel: Bad. Every time he speaks to us we don't listen to him. It makes us turn bad if you know what I mean. It like causes ... [I mean] he calls everyone a clown and only excludes Black people. He must think we'll react in a [certain] way to that. We're bound to react in a bad way.

(Chantel, Year 10 pupil, School B)

Chantel has responded to the way that she feels school exclusions and the tightening up of discipline have been racialized by the Headteacher. She has responded to the issue of exclusion in a way which was not gender specific. Indeed, some of the pupils in the study responded in a way which cut across their racial and gendered positions. However, Chantel and her friends, have employed racial signifiers (such as 'kissing their teeth'), as a means of empathizing with the African-Caribbean boys who experienced exclusion before them. Much research has also drawn attention to the issue of Black females responding in empathetic ways to the unfair treatment they feel their African-Caribbean male peers experience within schools (Wright 1985,

1987; Mac an Ghaill 1988; Gillborn 1990). Chantel and her peers have effected a homogenous response to Mr Mills which in a sense resists his attempt to both racialize and gender the issue of school exclusions. However, in the process of trying to address his own concerns about his Black pupils, and some of the pupils' worries, Mr Mills proceeds to give a particular identity to the issue of disruption and in doing so produces a set of 'excluded' masculine and feminine identities.

> 'A while back there was loads of tension between Black students and the teachers. They even set up a ... thing for Black students where Mr Mills was there, and another teacher and he [Headteacher] was like asking us why we was getting into so much trouble and stuff like this. And it happened once ... and then they said "oh this is going to happen every week". Then the students were OK about it, well not OK about it, we were quite annoyed because it was just like Black students ... He said it was going to happen every week, and we had one. And that was ages ago, and it's not happened again ... There was so much going on with black students that something had to be done ... The Black students were getting into trouble, getting a bad reputation ... The popular Black students, they seem to get in more trouble than everybody else, it's like ... if you're Black in this school, you've got to be quiet, like a good little Black person, you can't be popular. You're not allowed to be popular, and that's why they were getting so much trouble.'
>
> (Aaron, mixed parentage, Year 10 pupil, School B)

Mr Mills, in calling together a group of Black pupils, the majority of whom were male, felt that he had finally addressed the 'race' problem emerging in his school. However, the Black pupils who Aaron speaks of above, rejected being 'singled out' in their view by the Headteacher, although they did want a forum within which they could discuss their experiences. The Headteacher had racialized the issue of disruption and other pupils felt this negated his attempt to introduce 'discussions'. However, the Headteacher felt that his efforts had had a positive effect on his pupils, although the exclusion of Black pupils had continued throughout the term:

> 'The number of Black kids excluded has dropped right down. It will still be higher than the White pupils but again it's continued this term. Who knows what the reason is for that. I'd like to believe that as a result of that meeting that Black pupils feel we're concerned about them, that we don't want them to be excluded, whereas there might have been a perception before that that "they want to get rid of the Black kids, we're always being excluded". I just didn't know whether that was true or not. I was talking to [a senior teacher] and she thought the meeting was a very positive one but I think she felt it wouldn't be a good thing to give a sense of identity to a certain group of pupils who are selected out, as

being in danger of exclusion. Because it's a labelling process.'

(Mr Mills, Headteacher, School B)

The staff had felt the process of talking to the Black pupils about the issue of discipline and exclusion had been positive. However, the advice given to the Headteacher about the dangers of labelling a particular group of pupils suggested that careful consideration had not been given to the exercise. The meeting itself, and changes in school behavioural policy, had created tensions among some of the older Black pupils, because of the way that discipline and school exclusion had seemingly become racialized in general, and had targeted Black male pupils in particular.

In a similar process within School A, members of staff had begun to comment on the large friendship groups of African-Caribbean pupils in Years 9–11. The group began to give teachers cause for concern:

'I have noticed that we have ... the West Indian groups of lads grouping together as Black kids and running around. I say running because they are ever so gregarious ... of course you get White kids but they don't seem to be ... they [Black pupils] are always singing and dancing and they're much more physically expressive. Now that in itself makes them noticed more, and they're really keen on developing an identity. And there's a special uniform that they wear and if they can possibly help it, they'll get it into school ... they walk around with scarves across their face, with all of them [faces] hidden. That's fine, that's brilliant. Come into the classroom, coats off and sit down, but they'll bring it into the classroom. And we've got one or two of these groups with strong leaders who are actually coming out with the racist thing. Like "it's because I'm black that you're doing this." And that really irritates me because it's not, it's because they're not taking their bloody scarves off.'

(Mr Johnson, School A)

Mr Johnson suggests that the racial identities of these boys, and the signifiers associated with them (coats, scarves, etc.), prevented them from participating adequately in classroom interactions. It is also important to note that though the wearing of scarves in this way was seen by this teacher to have cultural currency for young Black males, scarves were also worn in similar ways by the majority of pupils, often being pulled up over mouths and noses. For the Black pupils in this group, the cultural currency was more evident in their abilities to group together within a predominantly White setting. The coats and hats worn were indicative of wider styles worn by African-Caribbean, and increasingly Asian and White, adolescents, in their communities.

What is finally important from the teacher's quote above, is that the discussion of racial identity is restricted to that of Black males. Within the same school, a friendship group of Year 10 Black females also existed alongside the male groupings. The response of the teacher cited above to issues of 'race' and the adaptation to schooling of Black pupils generally, appeared to begin with a discussion of Black masculinity. However, much of the above teacher's comments on this identity related to the group's separateness, which was perceived by the teachers as an act of resistance, whereas mixture was seen as more conducive to learning:

> 'They do group together, they want to have their own personal identity and that's how the uniform changes a bit. They wear woolly hats and we say no woolly hats in school, etc. and you have to keep on and on ... I suppose if they hang around together, it can be a bit intimidating perhaps for other kids. You know, we've got some other Black kids, lads particularly, who will just do their own thing. Hang around with everybody else and just, y'know, *mix in.*'

> (Mr Peters, School A)

The assumption here is that Black children who achieve well, have managed to integrate, and those who do not, underachieve because of the racial identity which is fostered within the group. One Black female member of the group was aware of the way she and others were perceived and it is likely that other members of the group were also aware. This characterized their response to the teachers and the sanctions used. They perceived the involvement of racism in some teacher's interactions with them, because their friendship groups were seen by these teachers in racially negative terms. Grouping together therefore in this way, served racialized identity functions, and also acted as a way of resisting the desire for integration which the teachers articulated. This was a challenge not only to teachers' attempts to control friendship groupings, but also at the wider social relations which positions the grouping of racialized individuals together as separatist. What was particularly interesting about the presence of these groups in the school was that the group of African-Caribbean females appeared to generate the strongest response from staff. They generally felt that both groups were quite intimidating, but whereas some members of staff were worried that younger Black boys would simply find joining the group attractive and thus be unable to achieve effectively, the young women were seen as particularly intimidating, although not likely to underachieve. Although the forms of alienation the Black male pupils experienced in School A were not as clearly reflected in their presence in the school exclusion figures, the friendship group and hence the intimidation associated with it, were constructed in the shape of the Black male pupil.

The Production of School-based Genders – the Case of Masculinity

The concept of Black masculinity has been used by education theorists to account for the experiences of young Black male pupils and their expressions of 'machismo' (Sewell 1997; Mac an Ghaill 1995). Other work theorizing on

Black masculinity has tended to include the supposed sexism, aggression and violence of Black males (hooks 1991; Wallace 1978; Mercer and Julien 1988; West 1993). This approach has suggested that Black men, in being denied access to the attributes of White male power, seek to reinvent identities which involve exerting power over others, often in ways which are violent and aggressive. However, not only does such a focus reinforce stereotype but also leads to a homogenous image of Black masculinity. It also fails to provide a useful way of theorizing the experiences of many of the African-Caribbean male pupils in School C. Although many of the young Black men interviewed both inside and outside of school had been excluded for fighting with their peers, very few openly discussed violent interactions, or talked about engaging in violent responses to their teachers. Interestingly, it was the Asian and White male pupils who talked about particular violent incidents and much of this related to their own perceptions and interactions with the Black researcher. However, within School C a particular culture of violence was present, but not only between peers, and not necessarily where young Black boys were the perpetrators.

'Being a teacher in this school, you're sorted. The teacher kept us all back for detention one day. This one boy walked out of the door [and] the teacher grabbed him. There are a lot of people who witnessed this, all of the maths class and people outside. The teacher got him in a headlock and then punched him in his head. Everyone saw that and it's no lie. Then this other teacher said "oh let him go cry to his mother". He was crying because it hurt him. Teachers shouldn't hit you like that. The whole class complained [but] most of the teachers who saw it themselves said it had never happened.'

(Ahmed, Pakistani pupil, Year 10, School C)

In this respect a teacher has committed an illegal act, as the law currently allows teachers to use physical restraint only to obstruct fights between pupils. Although Ahmed does condemn the act, he also points out that as the teacher was not reprimanded, despite the presence of so many witnesses, his behaviour has been legitimated by the school's response. Hence in Ahmed's view, teachers are allowed to do precisely what they want to their pupils.

Within the other participating schools there were incidents where a small minority of pupils may have been involved in extreme levels of violence. However, this always took place within each group. The pupils here had witnessed an act that they knew to be illegal and clearly wrong, yet the behaviour had been sanctioned by the school. It is then no wonder that the levels of pupil resistance in School C were higher than in any of the other participating schools. Shahid, who wished to avoid conflict in order to remain in school, was also involved in a potentially violent interaction with a teacher. Clearly some of the male teachers in the school felt that the most appropriate way to respond to some pupils was with violent interaction. Thus whereas Mr

Mills had shied away from confrontation with Nehemiah in Chapter 2, other teachers were demonstrating that it was necessary to regain control of what appeared to be perceived as a group of particularly undesirable pupils. Control thus became a heavily masculine – and in view of the context within which these interactions were situated – racialized construct:

> 'You know these teachers, I think they're [like] normal people who walk around on the street ... When they haven't got white shirts, trousers on, some of 'em got suits on ... some of 'em have got glasses on, they're all the same to me ... Outside school they're nothing. They're nothing at all. Inside school they're the teachers, but no teacher could hit me in this school, neither can they touch me. This teacher that touched me, he won't touch me again 'cause I'd break his fingers. Near the sports hall, he started poking me in my chest, like a dog, y'know. Whack, whack saying 'Don't you want to do P.E?' I said 'sir, I'm grabbing your hand now, and I'm putting it back there where it belongs. Don't touch my chest, speak with your mouth, don't speak with your fingers'. [Then] he just walked away.'
>
> (Shahid, Pakistani, Year 10 pupil, School B)

Shahid suggests that as teachers are the same as other individuals outside of school, the status and power they confer upon themselves is illegitimate. Though he also uses verbal interchange in a similar way to the other pupils in order to effect his contesting of teacher status, he also implies a threat of physical violence. Embedded within Shahid's response is an acknowledgement of the illegitimacy of the sports teacher's actions. Certain forms of physical contact by teachers as a form of school sanction are illegal within schools. Therefore Shahid cannot be rendered powerless by a teacher's response which is legally, as well as personally, constructed as illegitimate. Shahid's response is not constructed through 'race' but rather the nature of teacher power. However, it also signifies a symbolic confrontation between the racialized background of the pupil and the teacher. This is particularly clear when this is set, along with the other teacher–pupil interactions at School B, within the school's increased surveillance of Black pupils through the threat of school exclusion.

These two interactions illustrated the ways in which schooling masculinities were being produced by male teachers at School C. Whilst another White female teacher complained of feeling threatened by one of her Asian male pupils, the threat posed by African-Caribbean male pupils remained, as they continued to receive disproportionate exclusions. Black male pupils, and the forms of masculinity they were perceived to characterize, were often quite central in the discourses of threat, confrontation and violence used by other male pupils in the case study schools. Although the violent interactions discussed here did not involve Black male pupils, this should not be taken as suggesting that they did not take part in such activity. However, the atmosphere which began to emerge in School C did not occur in isolation of Black male presence. If we consider the response of Mr Mills to Nehemiah and his friends, outlined in the previous chapter, and the admiration Shahid had for their refusal to comply to particular rules, a threat of confrontation had clearly informed the Headteacher's reluctance to pursue the disobedience of the Black male pupils. The use of physical threat by some of the male teachers served as a useful reminder to those Black male pupils who posed the largest threat to teacher authority, that other means of reinforcing boundaries between teacher and pupils were available. The relationship between Mr Mills and his staff was not mutually respectful, thus in the light of what some staff saw as reluctance to impose sanctions, physical force was brought into use. Furthermore, processes which encouraged admiration for Black male pupils on the part of their peers became mixed with the fearful perceptions of them that were held by their teachers. These contradictions created a climate of confrontation and consequent cycle of exclusion.

Emulating Blackness

In order to look more closely at the experiences of Black male pupils in school, it is necessary to explore the processes through which young Black males experience their schooling identities when their relationships with others become predicated upon assumptions about the nature of Black masculinity. Theorizing around the construct of Black masculinity often mirrors common perceptions. Notions that Black men are excluded from dominant and White definitions of masculinity have been criticized for the way they deny agency and impose a concept of mimicry on Black men. Sewell (1997) writing on the forms of Black masculinity expressed by male youth in school, criticizes the ways in which writers on this theme have tended to position Black males. He objects to their situation, as excluded from the dominant positions of men within patriarchy, which leads them to reinvent violent, hypersexualized forms of masculinity (1997: 23). He suggests that '[w]hat has not been documented are the many different types of Black males who do not feel a need to mimic White patriarchy' (Sewell 1997: 23). Clearly, research on Black masculinity has indeed portrayed Black males as 'cut off' from patriarchy in similar ways to earlier research on Black identity, which positioned Black individuals – both male and female – as pathological victims who desire, yet cannot achieve, Whiteness (Mama 1995). It is as problematic to theorize Black masculinity as constituted solely out of aggression, sexism and violence, which results out of their exclusion from White masculinity, as it is to construct Black femininities as constituting images of matriarchs, jezebels and mammies where they too are excluded from dominant definitions of womanhood (Collins 1990). bell hooks questions the way that negative aspects of Black male identity are portrayed as particularly unique within the popular imagination.

> [w]hy is black male sexism evoked as though it is a special brand of this social disorder, more dangerous, more abhorrent and life threatening than the sexism that pervades the culture as a whole, or the sexism that informs white male domination of women?
>
> (hooks 1991: 62)

Therefore, it is important to situate the educational experiences of African-Caribbean males within an analysis of the interrelation between 'race' and masculinity. The danger is that this will relate the problems experienced by some young Black males in schools simply to the way they express their masculinity.

Black masculinities are subject to processes of symbolic exclusion from the power and status associated with White masculinity. Young Black men, however, also experience institutional exclusion in view of their disproportionate representation in school exclusion figures. As highlighted above, within one school at least, two male teachers had attempted to illustrate the extent of their powerful positions over pupils through the use and threat of physical confrontation. The masculinism embedded within this threat can also be seen as a means of illustrating to those groups of pupils seen by others as threatening (namely African-Caribbean males), that their behaviour would be curtailed by other means in addition to the use of school sanctions. As mentioned earlier, schools produce specific definitions of masculine behaviour to be channelled into the competitiveness needed to succeed academically, or in sporting activities. However, the increased exclusions from participating schools of Black male pupils, and the perception of threat which surrounded some of their interactions with staff illustrates how their masculine identities could not 'fit' within schools. The racial background of these boys was instrumental in these processes.

One example of threat and masculinity was exemplified by Mitchell, a 16-year-old African-Caribbean pupil, who had been permanently excluded from School C which he had just begun to attend since moving from the North of England to the Midlands. He and his mother had moved after his grandmother had died, as all three had been very close and they had found it hard to readjust after her death. He had received no prior warnings to his exclusion, had never experienced an exclusion in his previous school, and had been excluded immediately for an encounter deemed confrontational by his new French teacher:

> 'That particular day, the class was just laughing, everyone was running a joke,[2] no one was concentrating on what they were supposed to be doing. And because I was laughing the loudest, the teacher started to pick on me. Telling me that it was because of me that they were starting. He started telling people to shut up, and trying to be aggressive in the classroom so I was shocked at first. I just sat down. I didn't really say nothing. Then at the end of the lesson he let everyone out. Then there

was three of us, and he held us back in the classroom. Then as I went to walk through the door he stood in front of the door, he told me that I'm going nowhere. I said "sir the class is over" so I pushed past him and then that afternoon I skived off. They said if I had been there I may have been able to resolve it but because I wasn't there, I was expelled. I didn't do anything when I pushed past the teacher and skived off for one afternoon. I thought how could teachers just expel me just like that. Everyone knew before me, because as I came into school, I came in late that morning. There's a girl in my class who sits on the reception desk and she said "Mitchell what are you doing here?" and I was at school the day before so I was thinking what you talking about? And then I went to the place where you register to sign in late and the woman asked me for my name, and I said it's Mitchell Barrett and she started going mad like "oh no Mitchell!" Like an outlaw had just come in! But she wasn't carrying on like that until I told her my name. And she said "just wait here a minute" and normally they tell you where your lesson is and where to go. And then a person came and he told me that I'd been expelled. He said I had to leave the premises. Never been excluded before, nor suspended.'

(Mitchell, aged 16, African-Caribbean pupil, School C)

Mitchell had not felt the encounter with his French teacher to have been either confrontational, or worthy of a school exclusion. Mitchell's confrontation with his French teacher had consisted of him having pushed past him to leave the room. It is likely that this encounter was perceived as likely to develop into something confrontational rather than as being inherently so. In pushing past his teacher Mitchell's behaviour had become imbued with threat. In addition to this, the fact that other staff members had been alerted to his exclusion and hence reported on his arrival, suggests that a threat had been steadily emerging around his presence in the school ever since he started there just three weeks earlier. What is particularly revealing is that Mitchell himself interpreted the receptionists' behaviour upon recognizing his name, as similar to the reaction a person would have to an outlaw.

At another level, the threat of confrontation is indicative of the perception of young Black men by their White and Asian peers. This relates to the effect that wider definitions of Black masculinity have on others' opinions of young Black males (Sewell 1997; Mac an Ghaill 1994). The relationships between Black and White males are often imbued with envy, threat and confrontation (Mac an Ghaill 1994; Back 1996; Sewell 1997). The envy and admiration directed at African-Caribbean males by some of their White peers is situated within particular definitions of Black cultural forms. The mass consumption of African-American rap and R'n'B music by White youth and their processes of emulating Black (male in particular) styles of walking and talking, position Black males further into discourses which promote their stylistic superiority over others. Although Black males were the main targets of these processes of emulation they were not the only recipients. A Black female Section 11 teacher in School B had noted that some White children responded favourably to her, not necessarily because of her attributes as a teacher, but because of assumptions of her personality linked to her racial background:

> 'One thing I do find is that the White kids seem to find it's cool to have a Black teacher. I don't know why, I think their association with Black people, especially in White areas, is what they see on TV and it's normally pot and stuff like that. So there's something cool about it. I found it especially in London, but I still find it up here. They really try to impress you. Some work harder [or] they'll show you their clothes. They don't know what kind of person I am at all. I could be really stiff.'
>
> (Ms Henry, Section 11 teacher, School B)

Ms Henry does not distinguish between the gendered backgrounds of the White pupils who wanted to impress her, which may have allowed further insight into the processes which work to produce these forms of emulation. However, she does note that there were wider definitions of Blackness and Black identity which were being drawn on by her pupils. The nature of the emulation here was clearly not problematic for the teacher.

The response of one of the White male pupils interviewed in School A begins to shed light on the complexities involved in emulating and/or envying aspects of Black masculinity. Earlier in this chapter the comments of two teachers at School A highlighted their views of a friendship group of African-Caribbean male pupils. However, the teachers failed to notice that the more immediate and smaller peer groups of many of the members of this group were mixed, as there were very few Black pupils in the school. Richard, a White male pupil in Year 9, was friendly with a few members of this large peer group and had developed a reputation with other pupils in the school for his ability to emulate dancing styles which were compatible with a variety of Black musical forms. Although Richard was not old enough, his sister would frequent nightclubs where the majority of the clientele were African-Caribbean and the music played included musical forms such as Jamaican-originated ragga, soul and American rhythm and blues. Richard's friendship group, and musical tastes, illustrated that he had consumed the particular notion of 'cool' which surrounded these aspects of Black identity. What was particularly interesting was Richard's enthusiam and deep respect for Mr Cheatle, the Deputy Head:

Richard: He's like an ex-policeman. He's wicked. I like him, he's bad.
Researcher: What do you like about Mr Cheatle?
Richard: How he tells people off. He stares at them. He looks like an eagle hunting out his prey. He looks at them and you can never look him in the eye. And then you just bow. He walks round and starts shouting. It's like he's waiting to pounce on you

Callender (1998) has noted the respect shown towards Black teachers within schools based on a particular perception of 'strictness'. It was the potential threat of the Deputy Head's anger, and the perceived ability of the teacher to strike fear into the hearts of his 'victims' that so enthused Richard. However, Richard's perception of Mr Cheatle stood in stark contrast to that of some of the Black male pupils who had received sanctions from him (see Chapter 3).

For the young Black males themselves, the contradictions embedded within the responses to them of peers on the one hand and teachers on the other, created particular climates for conflict and confrontation. Within the schools young Black males were placed in ambivalent positions by some of their White peers and teachers. Ambivalent definitions of Black men exoticize them for sporting prowess, musical ability and representations of style, whilst simultaneously criminalizing those same attributes. What is problematic is that though some young people reject the definitions of Black identity being imposed upon them by others for their essentialist and often simplistic notions of Black people and their communities (Back 1996; Weekes 1996), some young Black men, such as those featured in the work of Mac an Ghaill (1994), Gillborn (1990) and Sewell (1997), live out and act upon these stereotypes. As mentioned earlier Mitchell was permanently excluded from School C for disruptive behaviour. After his exclusion from School C, his time in his new school (School B), had been problematic in some areas. Much of the time, this related to the perception of him held by his White male peers:

Mitchell: I think that White kids act worse [than Black kids] 'cause that kid that threw the fireball at the teacher was a White kid ... White kids tend to look up to Black kids because they think that they're all bad, they all do robberies ... They do things to impress us. That's why Lee did it, 'cos he was trying to impress me. He goes 'watch, watch this, watch this'. And then he did it. I was laughing.

Researcher: How do you respond to that?

Mitchell: I think they're bonkers! What they doing that for, getting themselves into trouble just to make me laugh?. ... respect them, but you're mad. 'Cause I won't be doing it for them. No way.

(Mitchell, African-Caribbean, School B/C ex-pupil, 16)

Mitchell had been placed in a particular category by his friend in relation to notions of machismo seen to be present in Black male identities. In addition to the multitude of images of Black men promulgated within the media and specific forms of Black popular music, which can inform others' perceptions of the group, writers have noted the extent to which these definitions are emulated by young White men (West 1993; Back 1996; Dyson 1993). Luckily Mitchell's response to his positioning within these stereotypical discourses was simply to reject them. Unfortunately, the ability of young Black males to create new male identities for themselves is restricted, and the process of symbolically elevating and/or emulating young Black men does not necessarily give them a more privileged place in the hierarchy of pupil identities. As a result of the actions of Mitchell's White peer Lee, Mitchell was excluded from the classroom and told to spend four days in the school's on-site unit. Lee received no sanction until he returned to school four days after the incident and admitted he had thrown the 'fireball'. It is important to note that within the context of the school, both Mitchell and Lee were as powerless as each other and thus Lee's elevating of Mitchell's status did not extend beyond their friendship. However, the teacher who believed Mitchell to have thrown the fireball acted upon a similar perception of Black male pupil identity, but without the elevation and envy. In a similar way, in the previous chapter Shahid spoke enviously about the way Nehemiah resisted the control of Mr Mills. Mr Mills, however, acting upon a similar stereotype of Black masculinity, interpreted the African-Caribbean boys' actions with fear. These contradictions combine to produce cycles of tension, confusion, cultural misunderstanding and ultimately exclusion for African-Caribbean male pupils. Mitchell had never experienced an exclusion prior to moving to School C. After his permanent exclusion from there and his admission to School B, he experienced various forms of exclusion, including withdrawal from lessons, time spent in the on-site unit and school suspension.

Avoiding Stereotypes

Although Mitchell had received a sanction based on a perception of his Black male identity, he was articulate enough to recognize the stereotypes informing the behaviour of his friend and his teacher. Mitchell knew that others perceived him as a particularly large and thus threatening Black male pupil but he enjoyed attending school and meeting with his peers and believed that he would leave school and attend college. As a confident young man who recognized the contradictions embedded within the way he was responded to by others, he adopted a strategy of coping which was to laugh at and hence resist racial and gendered stereotypes.

> '... most teachers have ... I dunno what they have really, but they think that all Black people do is steal things especially. ... not all teachers, but a lot of teachers, especially teenagers ... the way that they act ... you'll walk into a classroom and the teacher'll have her purse on the desk or something, and then she'll just put it in her drawer, or lock her drawer or something like that. Just little mad moves that they do. Just mad. It's like when I walk down the road and people put their door locks on, their central locking [They're] scared. I just laugh, I think they're mad, they're scared of little, little me? Alright, big me! But I'm not gonna do

anything. If I was gonna do something, then you should be scared.'
(Mitchell, African-Caribbean, 16)

In many cases new definitions of masculinity are created by young Black males and it is simplistic to argue that the masculinities which are constructed for them are unproblematically taken on board. Because of the racial harassment he was experiencing Johnny, aged 16, had transferred to School A in his final year of GCSEs. As with Mitchell, he had managed successfully to move beyond the stereotypes imposed upon him from without, but only after recognizing the extent to which he had incorporated and hence accepted them. Johnny had previously lived in an area where the British National Party was very active, and because his father had been fairly well known, Johnny had been subjected to a variety of physical racial attacks. This had become reflected in his behaviour in schools, where he felt that teachers were not supportive:

'A lot of teachers, sometimes they're scared of Black boys. My form tutor was scared of me, you could tell. I was probably big for my age and ... he wouldn't tell me to sit down and take my jacket off. He'd wait till I'd do it. He wouldn't ask for homework. If he told me something and I disagreed with it, he'd back down straightaway. And I took that to my advantage.'

(Johnny, Year 11 pupil, School A/B)

Johnny had employed forms of resistance in school, answering back and fulfilling what he felt to be teacher expectations of Black male behaviour. His actions, however, were also related to his experience of racial violence outside school. Though he was aware that similar stereotypes were in use at School A, he no longer wished to contest them:

'Over here, every Black person is a "rude boy", if they dress a certain way. That's how they [teachers] see them. Here it's just more blatant, probably because they haven't got much Black people in the school. Because when I came here I had long plaits and I kept hearing people say to me 'oh he's a rude boy'. So I cut it all off. Just to give me a new image and start afresh'

(Johnny, Year 11 pupil, School A/B)

The teacher's fear of Johnny had led to his exclusion from learning, as the teacher would not ask him for homework, neither would he be challenged if he had said something incorrectly. Johnny recognized that he was reinforcing specific racial and gendered stereotypes and in doing so was merely contributing to a general process of his own exclusion. It is unfortunate that not all young Black men who are subject to these processes of Black male identity construction are given the space to distance themselves in similar ways. However, even where young Black males are able to distance themselves from these processes, the coping strategies they employ to avoid stereotyping and conflict can often be detrimental to their own identities (Gillborn 1990).

Of course not all teachers build upon a negative stereotype of Black masculinity in their relationships with their Black male pupils. The extent to which stereotypes can have positive rather than negative outcomes for particular racial and gendered groups, however, remains open to question. For example, the perception on the part of teaching staff, that Black schooling masculinities embody aggression/confrontation, may lead to a desire to channel these presumed and negative characteristics into pursuits believed to be more *positive*. The father of a Black male pupil who had been permanently excluded from School C for fighting, suggests that his son was responded to by the teachers of his second school in the following ways:

> 'With some of the sports teachers, because of his size, they wanted him to play sport but he wasn't having that. Nicholas said ... I don't need to prove myself to you, so some of them actually did not talk to him ... they would ignore him. If they were going down the corridor, eyes to face, they would ignore him, they would turn their heads ... and then when I brought that to the school to say well this is not a healthy environment, it's supposed to be about education and social life is a massive part of it, teachers denied it. 'Cause a lot of them were afraid of him because he left the school, being, you know, a fighter ... and they probably felt threatened by him, so they put him down in other ways. And because he wasn't using his size to play rugby for the school, or football or basketball, he wasn't any good. It could just be a general misconception about Black men, that we're violent.'
>
> (Trevor, father of Nicholas, African-Caribbean, 17)

Where the other (more subordinate) masculinities encouraged within schools embody the competitiveness and aggression supposedly channelled into sport, they become more acceptable. However, the masculinities of young Black men who refuse to take part in one aspect of schooling identity (i.e. the playing of team sports), because they are excluded from taking part in other more academic aspects, have no place within the hierarchies of masculinity in existence in schools. Nicholas was a high achiever and on arrival at his new school had expected that he would have been able to continue to study to as high a level as he had achieved at School C prior to his exclusion. However, Nicholas found himself excluded from higher levels of learning.

> 'When I got there [the new school] I got there in the late part of the year. The top maths class was full. There's a girl called Margaret, her mum and dad were governors at the school and everyone used to know she was the cleverest girl in the school. Everyone used to rush around her

desk [for answers] and then people used to come around my desk. One time the maths teacher asked Margaret "Margaret, what's the answer? You're gonna get it right, but do you know this?" She [says] "No, why don't you ask Nicholas?" He just looked [at me] and he goes 'No, it's alright' and he did it [the answer] on the board. I couldn't get in the top Maths group. I used to think he was kind of a racist teacher really.'

(Nicholas, African-Caribbean, aged 17)

Nicholas perceived that the maths teacher did not wish to interact with him within the lesson, and related this to a particular form of teacher racism. In view of this encounter, Nicholas rejected the school (though importantly not the education that he could receive there) and did not wish to represent them in sporting competitions and activities. Once he was not prepared to become involved in the masculinized activities legitimated by male staff in the school, he was placed once more in the potential threat category. Nicholas' experience illustrates that even where Black male pupils are painfully aware of the processes through which certain individuals may interact with them, it is very difficult to move outside of the restrictive stereotypes which inform others' opinions of them. Although Nicholas was aware as to why his maths teacher did not encourage his learning, and the reasons that the school wished him to play in their sports teams, it was difficult for him to move beyond the actions of the maths teacher in order to gain the knowledge that he needed. However, painful as it may be, it was far easier for Nicholas to ignore and reject the behaviour of the White male teachers who would not speak to him in the corridors.

Conclusion

Work on schooling masculinities has explored the expressions of some Black male identities and the way these can often embody exaggerated hetero-sexuality, aggression and confrontation, either with peers or teachers. However, to restrict discussion of the problematic nature of relationships between Black male pupils and White teachers and male peers, to expressions of masculinity, can act to pathologize their identities and suggest that they are responsible for their own positioning. Black masculinities within schools are not restricted to confrontation and aggression, any more so than are other masculinities. Further, the male identities of some of the African-Caribbean boys were seen as potentially confrontational and the actions described by some of the Asian pupils interviewed, illustrates the complexity involved in the way schooling masculinities have been produced within the research. All of the young Black men spoken to in the study wished to achieve, but many, like Nicholas who was never able to gain entry to the top set in Maths, found themselves placed in lower sets and on-site and pupil referral units, because of behaviour and conflict with others. Research has shown that the alienation which results from this process places young Black pupils in cycles of confrontation and underachievement (Wright 1985, 1992; Gillborn 1990; Gillborn and Gipps 1996). For some of these young men, their exclusion from dominant definitions of masculinity and hence high status academic knowledge and power, did lead to reinventions of Black masculinity, but not necessarily in the form of sporting prowess and heightened hetero-sexuality as suggested by some masculinity theorists (Connell 1989). How-ever, the masculinities they developed, though clearly being influenced by the way other peers and teachers stereotypically perceived them, embodied a recognition of the undervaluing of Black masculinity. In view of the way Black men are constructed, it is problematic to suggest that expressions of Black masculinity are simply misdirected responses to their inability to attain specific White male identities. Rather, it is necessary to look at the complex responses of young Black men to the way they are positioned within particular definitions of masculinity. Such responses include both a reaction against these stereotypes by acting out what is expected of them and the painful rejection of stereotype in order to move forward. As Alexander notes:

> Most studies have, however, regarded Black masculinity as an *alternative* to social status, rather than as an *extension* of it. 'Black macho' has been portrayed, therefore, as differing in kind rather than degree from the wider gendered power relations within society at large ... It is, however, only within the context of wider power relations – and as an extension of them – that Black masculinity can be fully understood ... Black masculinity is then perhaps best understood as an articulated response to structural inequality, enacting and subverting dominant definitions of power and control, rather than substituting for them. Rather than a hostile and withdrawn entity [black masculinity] can be seen as a base for interaction and negotiation with wider society.
>
> (Alexander 1996: 136–7)

It is not suggested here that some Black males act in ways which require school sanctions, but it does suggest that their experiences within education should not differ from White peers and those Black females who also behave in similar ways. In the chapter which follows we will explore the differential nature of responses to Black male and female students and the forms of schooling masculinities and femininities which are produced in schools.

Notes

1 However, Gillborn and Gipps (1996) note that the educational achievement of African-Caribbean girls is only relative to that of African-Caribbean boys, and their rates of achievement thus continue to remain below that of some ethnic minority groups
2 This is a local term for misbehaving.

5 Gendering 'Race'

Introduction

In Chapter 3 a Black male teacher at School B spoke about being able to talk and empathize with African-Caribbean pupils. In view of his ability to share particular cultural understandings with some of his Black pupils this teacher could successfully diffuse potentially conflictual situations whilst maintaining a trusting relationship with the pupil. He found that he was able to engage in banter with some of the African-Caribbean pupils in the school that other members of staff had problems with. However, what was also clear from the teacher's analysis of Black schooling experiences, was that this was an empathy he largely shared with his African-Caribbean male pupils. This was clearly illustrated in the almost always conflictual interactions he would experience with one particular African-Caribbean pupil. This was a young Black female pupil who would spend most of this teacher's lesson standing outside the classroom. As far as this Black male teacher was concerned this young woman (who is featured below) was simply 'becoming a stereotype of the younger Black woman'.

There is no doubt that large numbers of African-Caribbean male pupils and, increasingly, their Asian counterparts are experiencing their school years as a time of confrontation giving them very little space to focus on academic achievement. However, there are also specific processes at work which, whilst enabling increasing numbers of African-Caribbean young women to gain high level examination grades (Gillborn and Gipps 1996), also position them as arrogant and aggressive (Collins 1990). Feminist educationalists have illustrated the harsh reactions young women receive in schools when they transgress 'traditional' boundaries of feminine behaviour through challenging teachers and resisting various forms of subordination (McRobbie 1978; Riddel 1989). The experiences of young Black women illustrate that 'race' acts to underpin the way they are responded to in schools (Mirza 1992), creating similar processes of teacher interaction to their Black male peers, but with gender-specific outcomes. In this chapter we explore some of the differences in the way young Black male and female pupils experience their school careers, and in particular look at the way they negotiate and respond to the threat of school sanction.

'Race' or Gender?

In looking at the responses to schooling of both minority ethnic male and female pupils, this chapter is building upon the work of Black feminists who have historically argued for the interrelation of 'race' and gender in the exploration of Black experiences (Mama 1995; Collins 1990). There is much scope within the area of secondary education for Black feminist analysis (Mirza 1992). However, for some Black feminists, the need to focus on interrelating gender and 'race' within education has meant rejecting the way that mainstream feminism has subsumed constructs of 'race' within those of gender when exploring female pupils (Bryan, Dadzie and Scafe 1985). In view of this it has been argued that:

> Black women cannot afford to look at our experience of Britain's education system merely from our perspective as women: this would be to over-simplify the realities we face in the classroom. For Black schoolgirls sexism has, it is true, played an insidious role in our lives. It has influenced our already limited career choices and has scarred our already tarnished self-image. But it is *racism* which has determined the schools we can attend and the quality of the education we receive in them.
>
> (Bryan, Dadzie and Scafe 1985: 58)

These are important considerations when exploring the experiences of Black female pupils in schools, particularly in relation to the way they may experience teacher stereotyping. However, if Black feminist perspectives are to be made integral to an analysis of Black female and male experiences within education, the complex ways in which gender and race intersect for Black pupils, require examination. This includes an acknowledgement that gender is not restricted to the exploration of femininity and therefore that sexism is not the only modality through which gender is experienced.

However, Bryan et al.'s (1985) comment above provides a useful starting point for an exploration of the identities of African-Caribbean and Asian pupils. First, it highlights the inadequacies of existing feminist analyses of girlhood, in view of their inability to account for 'race'. Second, it points to the prevailing influence of 'race' on Black experiences, and thus will be useful in interrogating understandings of Black femininity and masculinity in schools (Wright et al. 1998).

Black feminists for years have rejected the ways that Black female identities have been theorized within research as resulting in the primacy of either 'race' or gender (Collins 1990; Mama 1995; Brah 1992). There has also been much disagreement with the notions of 'triple oppression', and 'double subordination' which position Black women as victims of racism, sexism and class status. These definitions of Black female subordination imply that each aspect of self (race, class or gender) are static, independent, hierarchical and additive (Mirza 1992; Westwood and Bhachi 1988). Black women have been known to assert that their racial backgrounds are the greater determinants of their economic and social positions, rather than gender. And, as highlighted by Chantel in the previous chapter, though some teachers may respond to Black males in relation to their gendered and racial backgrounds, young Black women are often responded to in similar ways as their Black male peers. This chapter will not attempt to explore the different responses of Black female and male pupils to schooling through placing either 'race' or gender as the most important aspect of their identities. Rather, the chapter will seek to determine whether or not there exist differences between the way Black male and female pupils respond to school and, if so, the extent to which these differences (or indeed similarities) are related to the ways that schooling femininities and masculinities are produced.

Attempts to explain the differing adaptations of Black male and female pupils to schooling have been rare. Mac an Ghaill's (1988) study of teacher–pupil relations offered an analysis of the 'Black Sisters' – a group of high achieving African-Caribbean and Asian female students – and of the 'Rasta Heads' and 'Asian Warriors' who were male pupils at the school under study. Though that study provided a useful examination of gendered and racialized forms of pupil resistance, comparison was only made of the strategies adopted by the African-Caribbean and Asian males, since the 'Black Sisters' were older college students. But like the respondents in the work of Fuller (1982) and Mirza (1992), the 'Black Sisters' in Mac an Ghaill's (1988) study, highlight the fact that strategies other than disaffection are open to Black pupils. However, the experiences of the Black female members of this group were not looked at explicitly. Other work has suggested that due to the prominence of female-headed households within many African-Caribbean families, and the participation of Black women in the labour market, young black females acquire gendered identities which differ to those of both White females and Black males (Phoenix 1988). Such theorizing of gendered differences among Black adolescents has been used to explain differing adaptations and rates of academic achievement (Woods 1990). However, Mirza (1992) has criticized work which has attempted to explore the higher rates of academic achievement among African-Caribbean females, as often this work assumes that their motivation stems from their mothers' heightened commitment to occupational statuses, or, as in the work of Fuller (1982), suggests that Black females wish to prove their self-worth both to parents and to Black male peers. These theoretical assumptions position Black women within the stereotype of the 'superwoman', negate the experiences of Black females in families which are not female headed, and also fail to theorize adequately the experiences of Black males, through suggesting that they have negative attitudes towards Black female peers, or by reducing them to the status of absent Black fathers.

Differential Experiences

Very few pupils interviewed noted that any differences existed between themselves and their male peers within the area of response to school sanctions. For those pupils who voiced concern at the way they interacted with some of their teachers in relation to racial conflict, this very rarely pointed to any difference between boys and girls. However, one of the young women interviewed noted differences between male and female pupils. Samantha, an African-Caribbean, year 10 pupil in School A, was also a member of a large group of pupils, who would often mix with the group of African-Caribbean males mentioned in the previous chapter by the teacher from School A. Her response to staff perceptions of her group and Black pupils generally was both one of concern and one that berated Black male pupils for the way they would confront their teachers. Thus she saw her response as different to those of her male peers.

Samantha: If someone starts on us, we'll start back ... I think that's why the teachers have picked up on it. It's just got stupid now [because] if any little thing happens, 'it's those Year 10 girls'. Especially if there was a fight ... [and] all the Black people are together ... 'Cause some of them are Black, some of the teachers are intimidated by that as well because it's a big group and maybe they don't know how to deal with it or whatever. So the first instance of [anything] ... [they say] 'right get inside, something's going to happen', and that's the only way they can deal with it ... And like with the boys as well, they're like half-caste and Black. But they [boys] make it worse anyway cause, they just, they can't keep quiet, they just have to mouth off. They should just stand still and go 'hmm' *(imitates raising eyebrows at imaginary teacher)* and talk about it later.

Researcher: Is that what you do?

Samantha: That's the best way. Keep 'em sweet *(imitates slowly nodding her head to imaginary teacher)* and just like walk off.

Samantha realized that she was in a group which was viewed in a particular way by some staff. It is worth noting that the school had a small ethnic minority pupil population and many of these pupils were very close and spent much of their time with each other. Samantha also highlights that there are differential ways in which the African-Caribbean males and females respond to their construction as 'problematic'. Samantha felt it important to talk about interactions with teachers with her peers and family members, whereas she felt that the boys were too eager to confront teachers with their complaints. However, she would also engage in verbal interchange with subject teachers if involved in a disagreement. The Head of Samantha's year also commented on the behaviour of the group of girls with whom Samantha was friendly:

'Samantha is somebody who, at the moment, is giving me a lot of cause for concern. She's a bright girl. She's got a lot of potential. Causes an awful lot of problems with regard to friendships with other girls. Other girls can be at times quite intimidated and threatened by her. [She] has a little mafia-like friendship group around her, who when they move around school at times can make other children feel ... [She] has been involved in fights at times. I can see her being very intimidating to a new Year 7 pupil.'

(Mrs Frank, School A)

The group of young women who were part of Samantha's peer group had similar qualities to those of the young Black and White women called the 'Posse' in Mac an Ghaill's (1994) study. Pupils often reacted to Samantha and her friends on the basis of their reputation for fighting in the school, and Samantha felt that because of this, if another pupil attempted to provoke her, teachers would think them to be the innocent party.

'There's this girl called Emma, and me and her hate each other! Me and her had a fight one time outside of school, and she's got this thing where she's so paranoid and any little thing she'll run to the teacher, if I'm talking to her, she thinks I'm going to jump her again. I get told off for that and one of my friends got suspended. And to me that says we're targeted because ok we had a fight with her before and if we argue with her or any little thing she can run and get any one of us she likes suspended. And that's why I think that the teachers sometimes just jump on her side. [My friend] was arguing with her in the tuck shop and she [Emma] was arguing back but they [teachers] don't see that. She could start off an argument, if we argue back it's that person that gets punished.'

(Samantha, Year 10 pupil, School A)

It is of interest that Mac an Ghaill should consider that the group of young women in his study adapted to schooling in masculine ways. Connolly's (1994) work on masculinity illustrated that White male peers would attempt to provoke African-Caribbean male pupils who had 'fighting' reputations, in order to challenge their masculinities. The ability to fight in school therefore has specific masculine connotations. However, to equate the behaviour of Samantha and her friends with masculinity, reinforces specific 'controlling images' of Black women as 'non-feminine' (Collins 1990). These racialized stereotypes interact with those held by teachers generally of young women who subvert traditional definitions of femininity, as documented in feminist theorizing (Davies 1984). That the young Black women in this peer group constructed themselves in ways which led to them being considered 'non-feminine' (they would integrate the wearing of exceptionally short skirts with big coats, trainers and scarves) situates the nature of their response.

In this respect Mrs Frank and other senior teachers who had sanctioned Samantha and her friends in the past had constructed a particular form of femininity which Samantha found difficult to move away from. Samantha has an experience of schooling which is very similar to that of Nicola in the previous chapter. However, Nicola only ever engaged in particular forms of 'messing about' which she readily acknowledged, yet continued to experience surveillance out of proportion to her 'offences'. Samantha, and many of the young women featured in this chapter, were seen by senior teachers as quite 'serious offenders'. The problems of peer conflict which are found in schools throughout the country such as that which existed between Samantha and Emma, did require teacher intervention. However, these interactions had become translated over time into 'intimidation' in view of Emma's ability to draw on teacher assistance even in situations where it was not warranted. In addition to this, although Samantha and her friends would quite readily confront peers with whom they had developed 'problems', the extent to which Samantha would engage in verbal confrontation with her teachers was limited.

Researcher: How do you feel when you get into trouble like with these sorts of things?

Samantha: I feel frustrated. Because if you want to get your point across, like now we're talking, I'm explaining my point, but if you were a teacher it would be 'shut up I'm talking now' and you have to stand there and that's why I get mad.

Researcher: How do you cope with your frustration? What do you do?

Samantha: I just stand there and then I listen and then I'll just walk out. There's nothing you can do, if you open your mouth then it's going to get worse, so you might as well shut up and then just walk out. I'll talk about it to my friends or whatever. I'll tell my mum as well. And sometimes she'll ring up and complain because my sister used to come to this school and it happened to her and it's happened to me. Now my younger sister, she's [mum] not going to send her here because my mum doesn't like it. My mum was going to take me out of the school because she was fed up with it.

The 'hard' reputation which teachers had attributed to Samantha and her friends in relation to their grouping together, and the intimidation likely to be felt by other pupils, clearly did not extend to Samantha's interactions with school staff. Rather than continuing to give reasons for behaviour or to suggest that teachers may have misunderstood a particular situation, Samantha realizes that in her interactions with teachers she is relatively powerless. She therefore does not pursue the issue and in contrast to the responses of her male peers as outlined above, instead complains to peers and family members. It is difficult therefore to place Samantha's response as one which is inherently 'masculine' through her ability to fight well and earn a particular reputation, when the very clear power differential between herself and her teachers restricts her ability to resist teacher definitions of her. The power differentials between some of the male pupils outlined in the previous chapter and their teachers were also evident. However, the male pupils would either respond physically (Shahid), disregard teacher instructions and hence the power embedded within them (Nehemiah), or in recognizing processes at work simply laugh them away (Mitchell). It would be simplistic to define the responses of Shahid, Nehemiah and Mitchell as masculine and those of Samantha and her friends as feminine. Rather it is important to look specifically at those processes within schools, or society as a whole, that produce definitions of Black masculinity and femininity and which then inform the development of different pupil responses both to the way they are constructed and schooling generally.

For example, within School A some of the staff interviewed (such as Mr Johnson and Mrs Frank quoted in Chapter 4), felt that pupils grouping together ethnically was problematic. Thus the problem for these teachers related to the group itself regardless of the gender divisions within it. However, the teachers themselves, when asked about the relationship they had with their pupils from an ethnic background, would for the most part initially mention African-Caribbean boys only. As with Mr Johnson who was quoted in Chapter 3, another senior teacher felt that some of the Black pupils were likely to experience school differently to their White peers but only talked about the Black male pupils he had observed:

Mr Peters: We've got some Black kids, and they seem, not all, but a lot of them, to hang around with their own peers within a group. They have their own sub-culture. Try to bend the uniform so they can dress in whatever way and so when they're together, some of them don't perform as well as they should do, because, yet again, they want to be one of the boys. And they're bright, there's no problem in that respect, it's just they want to be different – that's understandable perhaps – but it does affect the way they learn. Perhaps they do see school differently to other people. Black lads, really.

Researcher: Lads more than the girls?

Mr Peters: Oh yes. There's no problem with the girls at all. Year 7 lads will come in, they will see the Year 9 lads and want to be a member of that group.

(Teacher, School A)

It is also necessary that the gendered and racial backgrounds of the teachers themselves be taken into account in the way that they may produce particular definitions of pupils. In Chapter 3 we noted the use of physical confrontation by two male teachers in School B as a form of maintaining discipline and control of wayward male pupils. These may indeed be extreme cases but the ability of 'good' teachers to maintain control in ways which may involve physical coercion has been noted elsewhere (Beynon and Solomos 1987). There may also be similarities between the relationships of Nicola and her teacher Ms Gotham, and Samantha and her Head of Year Mrs Frank. Whereas some male teachers may attempt to draw on stereotypical definitions of masculinity in order to effect control over male pupils, female teachers speak of female students in ways that male teachers would feel uncomfortable doing

> 'She [Rebecca] can be charming and equally she can be, if you'll excuse the phrase, a little bitch. At the moment she is against the system by being perpetually late with her skirt right up her bottom. When challenged about it [she] doesn't understand why you are picking on her.'
>
> (Mrs Frank, Head of Year, School A)

In School B, in contrast, Mr Shotter, an African-Caribbean male teacher had developed a supportive and often empowering relationship with some of those African-Caribbean male pupils who gave other teachers cause for concern. Despite this, he had experienced difficulty with Chantel, a Year 10 pupil. This had been noted by other teachers. It is interesting that other teachers who had clearly recognized Mr Shotter's success with his male pupils, were surprised at his 'failure' with Chantel.

> 'Chantel? Oh dear we hit if off really badly. I think her basic problem is her attitude. She's always right and no matter how many times you tell her she doesn't listen. I think she's becoming a stereotype of the younger black woman. Her whole demeanour. She's always arguing with you and playing up.'
>
> (Mr Shotter, School B)

Other staff who spoke of the difference between the Black male and female pupils Mr Shotter taught in the school, pointed indirectly to different teaching strategies that the male and female pupils may have responded to more positively.

> 'I don't know if it's luck or design but he captures this group because they're not given much chance to talk, yet he actually discusses things with them. He's really heavy handed with his discipline. He threatens them with thunder and lightning but once he's got them they're very happy and they talk to him. I wouldn't teach my class like that but it's up to Mr Shotter. He has them under control, though you see those kids elsewhere in school and they're total riots. The interesting thing is that Chantel has major problems with Mr Shotter. She'll come storming out

of the lesson and over here. I get the impression that she likes to chat and he's quite strict and perhaps she can't handle him shouting at her and telling her what to do. But she has a bad time with Mr Shotter and he has a problem with her. More often than not she's out of the room.'

(Ms Henry, Section 11 teacher, School B)

Mr Shotter felt more comfortable talking about some 'race'-specific issues with other Black males, and although there were two other Black teachers in the school, both were female, and he felt that the differences between Black males and females generally were too great.

'This is probably a sexist comment but these are male issues. Sometimes you want to talk to a Black man. Whereas if you talk to women you have to sit and explain. I know that it's a sexist thing to say but men do look at things in a different way.'

(Mr Shotter, School B)

Thus Mr Shotter's inability to 'control' Chantel was linked to a certain degree to his belief in the differences between Black males and females. He had attempted to try with Chantel but she simply did not respond well to his disciplinarian approach to teaching and as a result she became one that he simply had 'failed' to succeed with. Mr Shotter felt that using stricter teaching strategies worked with some of the more disruptive pupils and these pupils, the majority of whom were Black and male, responded well. Chantel, however, did not respond to these teaching methods which could relate as easily to her individual personality as it could to her gendered background. However, the fact that Mr Shotter's method of interacting with pupils was more successful with Black males than it was with one of the few Black females he taught, suggests that wider gendered processes were at work.

Power and Powerlessness

Samantha, who had developed a reputation equated with non-feminine behaviour, can be seen to derive relative forms of power from her position within the school. However, Samantha's inability to counter what she felt to be teacher misunderstanding, illustrated that her power was both relative and limited. The nature of the power or powerlessness that pupils experienced as they attempted to respond to the racializing of sanctions and exclusion was to a certain extent mediated through their gendered positions. As outlined below, often the young Black women would draw on particular responses to injustice which may or may not have been shared by their Black male peers. Their responses related to their status as pupils within school, viewed in relation to teachers and the school in general. But as Riddell (1989) has argued: 'for many pupils, education is experienced as a form of repression'

(Riddell 1989: 184), and the area of school sanctions made this power relationship even more evident. Many of the pupils in the study, regardless of their racial background, talked about the ways they attempted to subvert the traditional relationship of teacher as powerful, student as powerless. The responses of the African-Caribbean and Asian pupils showed their awareness that power was also mediated through particular gendered and racialized concerns. Therefore, it would be simplistic to assume that these pupils reacted against an unequal power differential without acknowledging the way that their own racial and gendered backgrounds affected their experiences.

As with Samantha, quoted above, and Nicola in Chapter 3, Chantel developed responses to schooling which incorporated various forms of resistance – using attitude, or wearing school uniform in a particular way – together with a recognition that their resistance could only go so far. However, Chantel was responding to the overall threat of exclusion embedded within the new discipline policy at School B. Due to both the increasing numbers of Black pupils who were experiencing fixed-term exclusions at the school, together with the recent report produced by the Headteacher around the aggressive behaviour of some Black male students, the classrooms and corridors had become racially charged. The few Black female pupils who were included in the research responded to the inherent powers of their teachers to employ school sanctions through highlighting their own powerlessness. It is important to note that resistance theorists have written about the responses of particular groups of students to their powerlessness within educational institutions for many years (Bowles and Gintis 1976; Willis 1977; McRobbie 1978; Giroux 1983; Davies 1984; Aggleton 1987). Pupils within all five schools, regardless of their racial background, reacted to their positions as pupils in relation to their teachers. However, the racialized tension within School B had placed an increased focus on the use of exclusion by senior members of staff and the possibility that a pupil may experience an exclusion here was perceived by African-Caribbean pupils to be greater for them. In the previous chapter Chantel talked about her relationship with her Headteacher. However, she also talked of a response where her interactions with staff made her feel powerless.

> 'She's [teacher] got a big problem. She said something racist to me. I can't remember the words but I reported it and [the Headteacher] says 'you'll find that Miss Beverage is not racist because she is in the Black bullying "group". Sometimes we just go in the [section 11] room and cry our eyes out. We just cry, because we report it, report it and no one does anything. So they wonder why we turn bad. [They say] "the best thing to do with Chantel is to chuck her out before the lesson starts". I go home and I feel like ... I've just started my period.'
>
> (Chantel, Year 10 pupil)

Chantel's response to tensions within her school go beyond the interchanges between staff and pupils so often seen by teachers as pupil inability to take responsibility for their behaviour. Chantel's inability to persuade senior staff of her concerns is one mediated through both her racial background and her gendered position.

'Me and Donna were in assembly and this White boy was talking. Miss Beverage came up [to us] and said "You two, out now!" Me and Donna looked at each other and said "What are you talking about?" and then she said we were talking and we didn't even say one word. Mr Mills [Headteacher] sent us to his office, gave us a detention and everything. But we wouldn't go because we didn't do nothing and we didn't say anything. So anyway they were saying that we were talking and everything and we just said "what's your problem? What's your problem with Black people?" and [Mr Mills] said "Are you trying to say we are racist?" We says "No. We're just standing up like fools saying it for no reason!" And Donna kissed her teeth. So he says "Don't think I don't know what that means" ... and he started shouting "get out of this school, you are going to be excluded" [We said] "... we haven't done anything wrong". Then Miss Beverage came out and we had two teachers shouting at us. We got punished. Donna got excluded and she had to apologize – for nothing, for nothing! Donna started crying when she walked out of his office because she was saying sorry for no reason.'

(Chantel, Year 10 pupil)

Both Donna and Chantel have reacted to their powerless status in the pupil–teacher/school relationship. It appears that the powerlessness embedded within their inability to convince the two teachers that they had not in fact been talking in assembly engenders an almost helpless feeling. They also avoid displaying this helplessness to the teachers who are sanctioning them. Chantel goes into a separate room, and Donna waited until she had left the Headteacher's office. Thus they attempt to extract power from the interactions with teachers at every available opportunity by verbally challenging decisions which they feel to be illegitimate.

Conclusion

This chapter has explored the differential responses of a small group of pupils to schooling. Though there were clearly some important gendered differences in the way Black pupils adapted to school, the more prominent differentials and similarities were based on 'race'. For example, the greater surveillance of African-Caribbean pupils (both male and female) in both schools, illustrated that the group was homogenized by teachers. Gendered differences were also evident. For example, Samantha's group of female peers were referred to as a 'particularly nasty group of girls'. Such a comment serves to underscore feminist theory, which points to the way in which female deviance is individualized and responded to on the basis of inappropriate femininity (Davies 1984; Robinson 1992). Regardless of this, however, the gender of the group became subsumed within their presence as challenging African-Caribbean students.

However, it was also noticeable that little reference was made to the Black female groupings in School B, and that the Headteacher here considered the African-Caribbean male pupils to pose specific discipline problems. Thus, the process of equating 'race' with disruption is not a simple linear development; it is based around the way that 'race' has historically been gendered in the image of the Black male (Mama 1995; hooks 1991; Wallace 1979; Mercer and Julien 1988). Teachers and schools which racialize (and hence gender) notions of non-conformity, disruption and school sanctions, contribute to the equating of 'race' with masculinity, which has important implications for theorizing how *all* pupils adapt to these processes. Clearly a Black feminist perspective on this issue might interrogate the extent to which 'race' is the prominent feature in Black pupil identities.

6 'Race' and the Social Consequences of Exclusion

Introduction

This section of the book develops many of the arguments around school ethos as discussed earlier in Chapter 2. It builds on these discussions to explore how the organizational culture of schools and their individual interpretations of a wider policy ethos, impact upon the rights of parents to gain an adequate education for their Black children. In taking up the issues raised by families affected by exclusion, the chapter moves beyond individualized accounts of inequality within schools, to also concern itself with schools as institutions with distinct organizational cultures. In doing so it acknowledges the wider social and political cultures within which the school resides, paying particular attention to the role of new managerialism in compounding the processes of exclusion. However, here we will take the survival techniques of permanently excluded Black children and their parents as the starting point from which to develop an argument around educational rights. We suggest that agency culture plays an essential role in the exclusion process and hence the creation of excluded identities and consider the extent to which certain factors appear to be a particular consideration in some schools' exclusion decisions and practices. Although not a major departure from earlier discussions, this section is based on the testimonies of 10 excluded African-Caribbean and mixed parentage young people, who are mostly male. It is also based on the attempts of their parents both to make sense of the educational experiences of their children and to provide a response which reinforces the fact that these young people do indeed have the ability to achieve and move beyond their exclusion.

An important aim was to include the parents and children fully as research participants. They offer explanations of the school disciplinary systems and the exclusion process and highlight how processes and outcomes affect their views of schooling. In doing so they have been given the opportunity to highlight the long-term impact that exclusion can have on life-chances particularly in relation to employment, and vulnerability to crime. This section therefore emphasizes the interconnectedness between the personal, social and cultural (Thompson 1997) dimensions in which the schooling of

African-Caribbean children occurs. It also explores how the negation of parental rights to secure education for their children occurs once an exclusion has taken place, and how the relationships between parent and school which form prior to and following an exclusion, can affect the whole notion of Black parenting.

Educational Rights

Increasingly, research on childhood and schooling has begun to focus on the need to promote children's rights within education (Whitney 1993; Osler 1994; Newell 1991) especially as through the experience of exclusion, those rights are denied. The present trend for focusing on the rights of children within policy (1989 Children's Act, UN Convention on the Rights of the Child) has implications for the way children are construed as users of particular services and institutions. As education plays a huge part in the socialization of children, many writers have documented the failure to acknowledge the rights of children to express views on all matters affecting them within schools (Whitney 1993). This becomes particularly relevant to the issue of school exclusions when it is considered that children are not made integral to the decision-making/appeals process as regards their education (Gersch and Nolan 1994; Allen 1994). Often, excluded children express the opinion that they have been misunderstood, or that their points of view have been disregarded or ignored. Additionally, children's rights can often become subsumed within those of their parents and in view of the effect of education policy on the relationship between teachers and more problematic pupils (Bourne et al. 1994), the parental interests of children who are not assumed to contribute effectively to the image of particular schools may not necessarily be served (Whitney 1993: 121).

The consequences of the denial of an equal right to education can be that young people no longer have the ability to participate fully in social life, and it is in this way that school exclusion becomes interlinked to that of social exclusion (Blyth and Milner 1994). That various schools may not be acting in the interests of the individual child (as outlined in Article 3 of the UN Convention on the Rights of the Child), as opposed to considering the interests of the majority of other pupils deemed to be affected by an excludee's behaviour, increases the possibility that time spent out of school without educational provision can lead to increased vulnerability to anti-social activities and/or criminal behaviours (Devlin 1995; Graham and Bowling 1995; Prestage 1993). Therefore the basic denial of an equal right to education, which emanates from the experience of exclusion, can have implications which extend well beyond the sphere of schooling towards 'the extent to which people can make effective choices, engage in decision making concerning their own lives, contribute to the quality of life in their community and have a voice in collective decisions' (Blyth and Milner 1994: 300).

Definitions of 'Rights' within Education

The concept of parental and children's rights within education has been much debated, and it has often been argued that the extension of rights for one group (parental rights of choice extending from ERA) have often occurred at the expense of the other (children's choices are subsumed within those of their parents) (Jeffs 1995; Whitney 1993). Those who are sceptical about the increase in children's rights discourses have often positioned these as indicating a reduction in rights for adults and thus '[a] popular misconception seems to prevail which believes that rights for children can only be won at the expense of denying rights to others; whether parents or the practitioners and people who work with children' (Franklin 1995: 5). Though the 1989 Children's Act was based upon the welfare of children in a variety of areas, especially in relation to child protection, it has been seen to take account of children's perspectives in ways which have not been repeated within education. The contrast between the right to consult the views of children within child protection and the failure to allow children to make representations at exclusions meetings and panels illustrates how 'educational legislation has always cast young people in the mould of powerless subjects within the system' (Jeffs 1995: 26). Children's rights thus have been seen as disregarded within education, because it is parents rather than children who have some access to decision making within schools. The increasing focus on children's rights exemplified in the UN Convention on the Rights of the Child, and the centring of rights of participation, protection and provision within it, have implications for the way that education is structured within the UK, as 'there is no duty to observe the best interests of the child in education legislation' (Newell 1991: 9).

Jeffs (1995) argues that the basic infringements of children's rights within schools can be situated within educational policy changes and the competitiveness, authoritarianism and individualism which emanates from this. The construction of the National Curriculum within the Education Reform Act 1988 and the loss of autonomy which teachers have subsequently experienced over lesson content, has impinged upon the rights of children both to select varied subject options and negotiate class content. Jeffs suggests that

> the right of children to a broad based intellectually stimulating education has been sacrificed on the high altar of competition. Refusal to offer young people choice and a measure of control over what they are taught produces conflict and disenchantment.
>
> (Jeffs 1995: 29)

Thus both teachers and pupils can become locked within a restrictive curriculum which both negates pupil rights and can often lead to disaffection, truancy or exclusion.

It has been suggested that in certain areas, however – access to education for children with special needs, for example – there has been an increasing interest in children's rights within education. For example, the improvement in participation of some 'of the most marginalised and disenfranchised group of pupils in schools' (de Pear and Garner 1996: 150) built upon the DfE Code of Practice (DfE 1994) which suggested that children should be directly involved in decision-making processes and exercise their rights to be heard on issues concerning them. However, this increasing involvement of children in decision making within schools did not until recently extend to excluded children. The increasing recognition of the effects of exclusion on children, and the rights of all children to an adequate education have been emphasized in work conducted by the Social Exclusion Unit (1998). However, in view of the persistent over-representation of African-Caribbean children within school exclusion statistics, it is clear that educational rights for these young people remains an issue.

Securing Rights to Education

The claim that the rights of children within education often become subsumed within those of their parents does not account for the experiences of Black excluded children and their parents. For example, the concept of choice formulated within moves towards open enrolment legislated within the 1988 ERA, are based upon the marketability of children. Those who are perceived as undesirable, either because of their failure to succeed academically, or because of anticipated behavioural problems, are often the members of marginalized racial and class groups. These constructs of marketability are recognized by the parents of Black children who have been excluded and the contradictions of 'choice' become clearer once Black children become involved within cycles of exclusion. In an interview with the parent of an African-Caribbean boy who had been excluded three times before, twice from primary school and once from secondary, and had experienced a fourth exclusion, his mother highlighted the discrepancies between choice as defined within educational policy, and that offered to certain parents:

> 'Anyway he got excluded again from [name of school]. I didn't have no say in the matter. From when he went in there anyway they were looking for him to fail. They didn't really want him there but because I applied and because the law is that I've got a choice, they had to take him, and they had to be seen to be helping.'
> (Collette, mother of African-Caribbean boy excluded for stealing from school office)

Though this parent felt that she did not have a choice in her son's exclusion, but had then exercised her choice to send her child to another school, this was then redefined as a theoretical concept (i.e. all parents can choose schools for their children) but not as a practical concept (not all children, or parents, may be considered eligible for the schools of their choice). The choice to select schools, and thus secure education for this parent's son was negated because he had acquired a negative status which appeared to act independently of him. The labelling of Black children as 'troublesome' has been well documented (Wright 1985, 1987, 1992; Gillborn 1990; Mac an Ghaill 1988) and though these within-school processes dictate the relationships which exist between teachers and pupils, once a child has experienced permanent exclusion, these racialized perceptions hinder the ability of parents to secure further education for their children (Blair 1994). In this way, both the rights of children to education and parental rights to secure this for their child become interrelated. Therefore for some parents, exercising their right to appeal against permanent exclusion at an independent panel does not similarly remove the possibility that prospective schools will interact with their child on the basis of his/her prior exclusion:

'Well I didn't like the way they excluded him. I told you I fought the exclusion and we won the case and as far as I was concerned he hadn't been excluded but he had obviously because it went to the next school with him and it's not supposed to go to the next school. And with that being on hand they knew Adam had been excluded and he was quite a difficult child ... but then with this business with the carrier bag hitting the girl in the face, he didn't get a chance. They just outed him straightaway.'
(Penny, mother of mixed parentage boy excluded for assaulting a pupil)

Thus although Adam's exclusion was eventually overturned his mother recognized that the effect of the exclusion had more of a lasting effect on Adam's educational career. Thus for some young people, experiencing permanent exclusions can signify that securing education within mainstream schools remains difficult or often elusive. Those who had experienced fixed-period exclusions understood how their educational careers would be affected by a permanent exclusion:

Mark: ... if you're really bad and you swear at the teacher and you lob your chair at them and all that, you get kicked out of school for that forever.
Researcher: Forever?
Mark: Yeah, expelled. Which will be quite hard. Like, if I got expelled forever, it would be quite hard for me to get into another school.
Researcher: Why would it?
Mark: Because when you get expelled the record goes with ya.
                       (Mark, excluded for being disruptive in class)

Clearly then, exclusions from one school can often indicate the possibility either of exclusion from other schools, or failure to secure a place in mainstream schools at all. As Blyth and Milner (1993) have argued, some of the main consequences of exclusion for a child are that they 'simply disappear from the educational system. Relatively few permanently excluded pupils appear to be provided with a place at another mainstream school. Headteachers appear to be increasingly reluctant to accept pupils excluded from other schools' (Blyth and Milner 1993: 257). And as one of the parents pointed out in relation to the effect of exclusion on her son:

Penny:　　　He's finished now anyway. He's got no life. As far as schooling's concerned. Where could he catch up now? He's 15 in September and when do they leave school? He'll never fit it all in.

Researcher:　You thought that he might go to college didn't you?

Penny:　　　Can't see him. No.

Researcher:　Do you think he'll just go for a job?

Penny:　　　Nobody would employ him.

Researcher:　How does that make you feel when you think of all that?

Penny:　　　It's annoying 'cause he's not got anywhere. I mean at the end of the day, all he was, was a kid that was quite disturbed. Nobody would help him. I gave more help myself really and because of all I went through, if I'd realized then what I know now, I'd probably try to handle it that bit better, but you don't do that do you when things is happening to you?

The extent to which children and parents can exercise control within situations of school exclusion are thus restricted. When parents have attempted to exercise their rights to secure education for their children, and thus have a degree of control within an area where both they, and more specifically the excluded child are rendered relatively powerless, these rights become subsumed within the quite intimidating processes of appeals panels or meetings with headteachers. This parent of a child who was about to be excluded did not wish to attend the exclusions meeting alone and arranged to have a local community worker attend with her:

'First of all, to be honest, Clive [the local community worker and advocate] was on holiday and they wrote to me and said I had to come to this meeting very, very quickly and that if I didn't come – 'cause I rang them to say it was inconvenient because I didn't have Clive with me and I didn't want to go on my own – they said that they'd go ahead without me. So I rang up somebody at [the education department] who attended the meeting ... he told me to put something in writing to them to state that I was unhappy about the meeting going ahead and I wanted it rearranging ... which is what happened and it didn't go ahead and then it was rearranged for me and Clive to actually be present. But they did try and sneakingly get the meeting to go ahead and they also knew Clive was on holiday because he'd told them two weeks prior. But the way they told me ... they made it sound as if there was nothing I could do, that they were within their rights to do so [but] no, this guy told me otherwise. He first said I had to put something in writing because I think he felt that what I told them over the phone, they could say otherwise.'

(Lorraine, mother of African-Caribbean boy excluded for unco-operative behaviour)

These experiences with the schools do little to increase the trust parents have in the schools where their children are being educated. Lack of trust in the school and teachers can further lead to conflict between Black parents and schools and determine future relations between them. Often the relationship between parents and school is influenced by their own past experiences of schooling which were at times quite negative, creating barriers to the forming of more positive and supportive relationships.

Déjà vu – Learning from the Past

The parents in this study all of whom experienced some or all of their secondary schooling in Britain, were well aware of the changes which had occurred since their own secondary education, and were quick to compare their own schooling with that experienced by their children.

'Years ago you had to do something really really bad in order to get excluded but now you don't really have to do anything.'

(Bernadette, mother of Shante, fixed-period excludee)

'Teachers have no tolerance of the kids no more.'

(Mr Bowman, father of child excluded from classroom)

'If there's a physical altercation, then the police are brought in straight away. [Today] Police are called at the drop of a hat. If teachers aren't taught to deal with things the children are going to be criminalized. Black boys are bigger nowadays, and Black boys' behaviour is misconstrued as aggression.'

(Trevor, father of Nicholas, permanent excludee)

The parents often made sense of their children's experiences by referring back to their own experiences of schooling in Britain. One mother often spoke with her own children about her experiences of racism during her school years and was eager to alert them to the problems they might face. All of her brothers and sisters rebelled as a result of the problems they faced and she returned to full-time education in order to gain the education she was denied the first time round.

'Every single one of my brothers and sisters rebelled as a result of what happened ... Martin's experiences are similar to what I went through. When I was at school loads of the teachers were racist ... one called me a Black bitch at school – the teacher was suspended on full pay and returned later for it ... was never to be spoken of again but I never felt the same again. I played truant and didn't take any exams. I was educated as an adult.'

(Miss Stewart, mother of Martin)

In light of their own experiences of school, choosing a school for their children was a very serious business for the parents in the study. Here again the notions of parental choice were fraught with problems as the effort to secure a place in a 'good' school often meant that compromises had to be made. Many highlighted the fact that they had to balance the educational opportunities extended by suburban schools with the isolation and particular types of racism, which they knew their children would face in such establishments.

'Everyone says that [Shante's school] is a brilliant school. For White – yes, but for Black it's a different kettle of fish. Every time I go there I see a Black pickney sitting in a corner because they do something. There's only a handful of Black children in the school.'

(Bernadetter, mother of Shante)

Though schools situated in areas with very few minority ethnic residents may not consider racism or multicultural education to be an issue, research has noted how the views of some young people and teachers can remain unquestioned, often given the fact that very few will have had any contact with minority ethnic individuals. In one study 'openly racist attitudes among pupils were being ignored by many teachers, who were unsure what racism was and tended to label such incidents simply as teasing or bullying. Teachers as well as pupils were found to be using racist language in the classroom' (*Guardian*, February 1999: 7).

The absolute and proportionate numbers of ethnic minority children within any school alters the cultural dimensions of the organizational culture, with inner-city teachers generally expected to have a greater sensitivity to diversity and an ability to respond to it. Where schools had less than a certain amount of ethnic minority pupils, parents were acutely aware of the problems which their children might face including exclusion. In such situations the students and their parents gave more examples of isolation, lack of sensitivity and ethnocentrism (see also Nehaul 1996). That ethnocentrism often resulted in poor responses to clear cases of need.

One student talked about the silence which accompanied his first visit to the school canteen. Students and staff stopped what they were doing and his maths teacher's mouth fell open whilst the food he was eating fell onto his plate. The headteacher admitted to Nicholas' father that he too had fallen silent when he first saw this new student and now recognized that his feelings had been badly hurt. This isolation never left Nicholas during his stay at this school and was frequently compounded when numerous Year 7 children would cry whenever they saw him.

Social Justice and Responses to Racism

The government intention was that a permanent exclusion from school should only be administered in the last instance (where other options have been exhausted or deemed inappropriate or ineffective and where the child is likely to endanger the education or welfare of others). The DfE (1992) found that the main reason for the exclusion of children was disobedience, such as refusing to obey rules, insolence and verbal abuse towards teachers. It would therefore seem pertinent to explore the situations in which such behaviour might arise.

The students who responded to this study attested to the extent of the everyday personal and institutional racism they faced. It would therefore follow that unless teachers are willing and able to address the issues of racism, then Black students will continue to get caught up unnecessarily in disciplinary processes. Certainly the evidence is that the schools involved have a tendency to deal more harshly with physical retaliation than with the many forms of racism which precipitate it. Left to their own devices African-Caribbean children, (particularly boys) tend to respond to racism inside and outside school on the basis of their personal and parental value systems. Although well aware of the power discrepancy between pupil and teacher, Black pupils and parents argue for equality of status between them in human terms. This is a source of great contention, and reflects a difference in opinion between the schools' and parents'/students' definition of equality. Many African-Caribbean parents expect their children to defend their 'racial' and cultural heritage, if necessary by physical force. Schools do not, however, accept this as legitimate behaviour, and two of the respondents were excluded for responding to racism in this way.

> 'I bring up my kids so that if anyone calls them racist this or racist that or Black this or Black that, or pick on you for no reason, you lick them down. I don't give a damn, I send them to karate every week for that same reason. Not only in the sense that someone can call you Black this and Black that and you brush it off. At his age I don't want him to be doing that or you could be brushing it off at twenty-five and that's not good. You have to put a stop to it, you have to know that you did fight and that you put a stop to it.'
>
> (Mr Bowman)

Lloyd-Smith's (1993) findings in this area are particularly relevant. Over 50 per cent of the complaints made to the racial equality council in Birmingham in relation to exclusion were made by parents of Black children, and in all but two cases the violence was as a direct response to racial abuse. Racism is a major factor in disruptive behaviour (Kinder et al. 1996a, 1996b; OFSTED 1993).

Mrs Stoddart and her family experienced racial abuse upon moving into the local authority area. In certain parts of the county, racism was experienced by minority ethnic residents as an organized and regular occurrence. Where young people may not have responded to a direct case of racial abuse leading to an exclusion at school, they often lived and socialized in areas where racist abuse was widespread.

> 'One night the Nazis with the NF came with guns, bottles, knives, chains to my front door. This happened for seven months. They sent letters to my door saying I was on their death list, letters about what they were going to do to me. I even got police protection. It affected all the children. Stephen went to pump up his bike tyre; this white man was using a pump on his car. Stephen told him to 'hurry up' and the man called him a Black c***. He hit the man and the man called the police. He fought the police. If it was [a larger city] the man would be dead because he wouldn't have a chance to call the police. The judge said it should never have got to court, when he heard what the man had called Stephen. But Stephen needs to learn to control his temper because there are ignorant people. He responds to lack of respect from others – we don't stand for any rubbish.'

It is not known how far conflictual relationships between parents and the school exacerbate the existent relationship between pupil and teachers which may have led to increased contact between home and school. Blair's (1994) research on Black families of excluded pupils documents the sense of powerlessness that many parents experienced against teachers, and head-teachers were often perceived by parents as exacerbating the likelihood that their child be excluded from school. However, the consequences of parental alienation from involvement within schools can have serious implications for excluded children where 'parents concerned expressed a sense of deep disillusionment with the system which they felt was weighted so heavily against them that to attend an exclusion "hearing" was not only a waste of their time and energy but was likely to have further negative effects on their already battered emotions' (Blair 1994: 47). Bernadette, whose older daughter had also experienced fixed-period exclusions from school, expressed worries about the way her son was supported at school. She felt that he was channelled too readily into sporting activities and that the same enthusiasm was not given by teachers to his academic work. Thus she would confront teachers about this discrepancy in the support her son received and it was upon such antagonism that her relationship with the school was based. Much of this was thus reflected in the exclusions meeting following her son's exclusion for fighting outside school (in front of his home) whilst wearing school uniform:

Researcher: So how did you feel when you got the letter and found out about the exclusion?

Bernadette: I was angry, I was angry 'cause I even threatened the Headmaster, and I gave him my report what I wanted him to do. I told him that since that happen I want a report that you make sure my children go on the school bus, reach my front door and come in, you're responsible for that. He says 'we can't do that' I says 'well you're telling me you're responsible for outside school 'cause they've got their uniform [on] so you've got to keep to that rule' ... and I just put him in his place ... I was angry because I got a letter to say he was excluded but they didn't give me the details and I was angry with Shante 'cause I thought Shante with his stupidness, 'cause all parents would think that [it's] your child just mischievous again, and a just cause problem, but when I actually went to the interview and they told me what went on, that's when I was fuming ... and I argued with him 'cause they still put Shante on a report ... and not just that but the headmaster was using his position to try and ... 'cause he's got his position he wants to use it to control us with it ... he was like, because he's the manager as they put it and in authority, he was using his position saying 'well I could use my position to do such and such, if I don't want Shante in the school I don't have to have Shante in the school' ... you know them words he use, them posh words ...

Bernadette's anger towards the Headteacher was based not only on her past experience with the school, but also on her perception that her son had been excluded for a trivial offence. The fact that her son had threatened a boy from another school who had called him a racist name was overlooked by the school, and it was this disregard for the way Black children respond to racist name-calling (Bourne et al. 1994) which also affected her negative relationship with the school. The maintaining of the image of the school (the Headteacher's decision was based upon the incident occurring whilst Shante was in school uniform), over and above that of the interests of individual students has been described by Jeffs (1995) as an overriding necessity to ' "persuade" staff and students to display total commitment (rather like the employees of a hamburger chain or Disney World) to the school's Mission Statement: every contact with outsiders is judged to constitute a marketing activity and opportunity' (Jeffs 1995: 30). Thus not only has the current ethos existing within schools constructed specific pupils as (un)marketable, which can subsequently affect the nature of the relationship between parents of unmarketable pupils and teachers, but can also allow the redefinition of events to be interpreted in relation to the effect unmarketable children may have upon the overall image of the school.

The ability of parents to exercise their rights to secure places for their children within educational institutions once a child has been permanently excluded, is further problematized where the parent is unhappy with the *quality* of education their child receives. Much research on exclusions has documented the problems faced by children whilst they are out of school and are thus not receiving educational support (Blyth and Milner 1993, 1996). But this overlooks the issue that parents may not wish to return their children to institutions where they do not feel them to be receiving adequate schooling. The two parents mentioned below both shared a view that the content of the curriculum taught to their children was not interesting, because it failed to reflect aspects of their own culture. As Bernadette argued in relation to the overenthusiasm she felt was shown to her son's sporting abilities:

'To me they not supporting him in his education, his academic education. Sports, they're quick fe do anything for him and to me personally, me tell him already "me never bring you in the world fe kill out yourself run for neither no school, nor country, no nothing, right?" And I prefer he knew more about himself, where he's coming from. He don't need to know about no blasted Henry the eighth and Mary this and Scot and ... they got nothing to do with him. He needs to know about himself ... He needs Black people, what they do, and what they achieved, and he can walk and be proud of himself.'

The increasing importance of additional classes both in mainstream, and supplementary schools focusing on the achievements of Black people throughout history (Yekwai 1988), is often an option selected by parents who wish to exercise their rights to secure a useful, relevant and interesting education for their children. As Jeffs (1995) outlined above, the inability of children to exert some control over the content of the curriculum can often lead to disaffection, through their perceptions that the material taught to them is of little relevance. This view was also shared by Annette but was articulated in relation to her decision not to appeal against her son's permanent exclusion from school as she did not feel that this school was the best environment for him. Thus exercising a parental right to a good education for children can be as much about a child receiving *adequate* education as it is that places in schools are available to them.

'I didn't appeal because I felt it wasn't in Andrew's best interests to try and get him back into that school. I felt ... that maybe what I have been overlooking as a parent is that Andrew is of the age where he needs a different environment and because of the things that we have talked about and you know the sort of reaction he was getting from the school and the teachers, I felt that environment would not have helped him anyway so what's the point trying you know, I had to safeguard his interests in the long run ... I think he was getting bored with the system

... with the curriculum. Personally, I feel that it wasn't challenging enough for Andrew and I'm not just saying that off the top of my head. I feel that Andrew been a child that ... he's very bright, he likes a challenge, you know, Andrew's left from here he went to boarding school in Jamaica and Andrew excelled ... but he's not academically challenged [here], whether it's right or wrong, whether Andrew needs to check himself or not, the fact still remains that he's not challenged within the school and he became bored with the education system.'

(Annette, mother of African-Caribbean boy excluded for fighting)

Annette illustrates that though the right to appeal is important for parents who want their child to remain in school, it can pose problems to have a child return to a school where he/she has initially been rejected through exclusion. Sharon, the mother of Paul who was excluded for stealing a chip from a computer from School C, also refused to appeal the decision to exclude on similar grounds. Although Sharon did not contest that Paul had been wrong in his actions, she did not feel that the exclusion had been handled correctly. Paul had been arrested on the spot and she had not been contacted until he had been at the police station. The school then said that he had been excluded for a fixed period which finally became a permanent exclusion without him having returned to the school.

'We didn't appeal because I didn't want Paul to go back into a school like that. I decided to direct my energies into getting Paul back into education. His behaviour changed for a while and he became very bitter and he regretted deeply what he had done. It deflated his ego and he felt let down. Parents should have a say in how their children are educated and who educates them. We don't know anything about the teachers forming judgements on our children but they want to know everything about them.'

(Sharon, mother of Paul, African-Caribbean, aged 16)

The media focus in recent years on teachers unions threatening strike action when children have been returned to school following exclusions appeals, emphasizes quite clearly the implication of this parental right on the excluded child. It may be here that tensions between parental rights (of appeal) and what is in the best interests of the child may arise, but at the basis of parental decisions to appeal or not, is the desire to secure the rights that their children have to education.

In terms of the parental rights offered by educational legislation, support (in terms of allowing parents the facility to choose schools and appeal exclusions decisions) is central both to official and parental discourses of what should constitute the rights of parents. However, the decision of some parents not to exercise this right in the best interests of their child, highlights the discrepancy between the way it is defined within educational policy and how it is defined, and experienced, by parents. Support thus cannot be limited merely to extending to parents the right to appeal an exclusion, as doing so can be both a very isolating experiences for a parent (who may not know where to seek personal support) and have implications for a returning child.

Power, Culture and 'Racial' Misunderstanding

The social relationship between pupil and teacher is a complex one, which is culturally specific. Indeed the depth of this complexity has been expanded upon in Chapter 3. During the interviews most of the students recurrently referred to unacceptable teacher behaviour, particularly in relation to the ways in which they were spoken to and approached. Respect had to be earned and this needed to be placed within an understanding of culture and ethnicity. In the absence of respect and the continuing rise in exclusion many pupils and parents argue for Black teachers.

Several parents said that White teachers could not manage and therefore could not educate Black children who they failed to understand. They believed the difference in culture to be too great for them to learn and that what was needed was Black teachers. There was no substitute.

> 'The exclusion was not fair or justified. They don't understand how Black people behave when they are frustrated by not being able to do something.
>
> You have to understand Black people's culture first of all before you can like judge or put down a Black person. Because they take it personal, they take things to heart ... and that is what the school does ... A teacher will talk down to Eton and Eton will hate that teacher ... anybody talk down to him .... you talk down to him that's it. I don't think that you have a right to talk down to pupils.'
>
> (Collette, mother of Eton, permanently excluded four times)

The students and their parents are aware of and live their lives in an environment, which is racially hostile and they have come to think about and respond to racism in certain ways. The nature of the responses from the young people in the study illustrated that as African-Caribbean pupils mature, they refuse to accept behaviour they perceive as being disrespectful, be it either from teachers or other peers.

Insiders and Outsiders: Black Pupils, Black Parents and the School

The stereotyped ways in which Black pupils and their parents are perceived by teachers inevitably affects the ways in which they are related to as service users. Black parents are often viewed as either being extraordinarily volatile and oversensitive, or as having little to no interest in the educational progression of their children (Tizard et al. 1988; Brah 1992; Wright 1992; Vincent 1995; Crozier 1996; Runnymede 1998). Indeed the idea that Black parents were not sufficiently concerned about the educational needs of their children was implied by several teachers. One parent complained that teachers had made it obvious that they disapproved of her decision to pursue a second-chance educational opportunity given her child's disruptive behaviour at school.

> 'They don't feel that Black people should achieve especially as I was not married and have seven children. They think I should sit on my back-side.'
> (Bernadette, mother of Shante)

A Black father found that certain assumptions were made about relationships within African-Caribbean families. The father found that when he tried to intervene in the exclusion process he was denied access to information; this was because the school presumed that he had no contact with his son. This was contrary to the actual situation as not only did the father have regular contact with his child, he also took major responsibility for dealing with the exclusion. He also looked after his son throughout the first temporary exclusion, setting and marking homework when none was received from school.

Education, Education, Education

Without exception the pupils and the parents in this research expressed a deep and consuming passion for credentials and education. All of the interviewees identified a future career and saw college as part of the process they were intending to go through in order to achieve it. Mirza (1992) found that the girls in her study were situated within a community of people who valued education highly with a commitment to achieving academic potential. Similarly all parents without exception took steps to support their children during the threatened expulsion and in the furtherance of their educational career. Every one of them on learning of the threatened exclusion visited the school, responded to the exclusion letter, attended the exclusion meeting. Many took the case to appeal. Where the school successfully permanently excluded their child and the parents' appeal was fruitless, all parents sought out alternative schools. Many wrote letters, two took the problem to the press (local and national), others sought support and advocacy from a range of community agencies, and not one simply took the problem lying down.

> 'I went everywhere, I got 'The Voice' [newspaper], The [local evening newspaper]. I wrote to the Director of Education. They never helped me and my Eton. The system failed us. I went to appeal. Eton is the ultimate victim and they just wanted a scapegoat.'
> (Collette, mother of Eton, permanent excludee)

109

Exclusion from school stands in stark contrast to the long-term aims of the African-Caribbean parents, who place such high value on the achievement of credentials. Exclusion quite obviously jeopardizes educational opportunities and future prospects for obtaining credentials. This goes some way to explaining the depth of feeling expressed by both parents and children following the exclusion. The participants revealed feelings of despair, isolation, loneliness and depression as a result of the exclusion, and were clear that the consequences of exclusion from school could have a lasting effect on the future of the excluded pupil. The following statement was made by a parent who had been forced to move several times in recent years and found herself and son homeless at the same time as grieving over the death of her mother.

> 'When I heard, I was devastated because we are just getting on our feet. I tried to get in touch with the teachers, they said they'd already made up their mind. I don't think he should have been excluded; it was barbaric. I asked them not to throw my child out of school, I am still grieving [her mother died close to the time of her son's exclusion and the school was informed of this] I was crying, but they seem to be saying – "this is how we crush people when they break the rules, and your son has broken the rules".'
>
> (Violet, mother of Mitchell, permanently excluded from School C)

The problems of managing the child's exclusion compounded the stress already faced by the family (Cohen et al. 1994).

> 'It's upset me a lot, I have to be here when the tutor arrives and I have to ring every hour to make sure he's ok, until his father gets home. I'm depressed and have to call my other son to talk about it. We have a good relationship me and Anthony, he's a good lad. He gets blamed for things he hadn't done from taking blinds down to setting off fire alarms. He got a bad report from junior school and it followed him to School C. They felt he had disruptive behaviour. The junior school failed him from the beginning. Once a Black child has been labelled that child is labelled for life.'
>
> (Juliet, mother of Anthony)

Parents often despaired of their child's situation following the exclusion and whilst they agreed that their child should be punished by the school for their misdemeanours, what they wanted was equal and fair treatment not based on 'race'. Indeed parents would often dissect the situation, identify and apportion blame to both the child and the school and punish the child accordingly. Should schools behave justly, then these parents would provide the utmost support to schools in the management of their child's behaviour and education.

Parsons et al.'s recent work (1997) considers the cost and other ramifications of school exclusion. This research considers ways in which the effects of exclusion fail to be restricted by time or organizational boundaries. Most notably the study concludes that the damage caused by exclusion seeps beyond the individual child to envelop the family, the community and wider society. For example, exclusion impacts upon the child in terms of lost education and future work prospects, as well as their relatives who become vulnerable to stress-related illness and family breakdown. Although some students stated that they were happy to have a break from the unrelenting pressure of daily racism, most expressed concern with what had happened, identifying a state of anger and bewilderment. For those who were excluded on a permanent basis and where there were several months between exclusion and a new placement, signs of depression soon followed. Stress was a major consequence of exclusion in the families who responded to this study, and the relationship between children and their parents was one of the first things to alter.

Researcher: Did his behaviour change [following the exclusion]?

Bernadette: Yes, he is not the Shante I know. He now has an attitude problem, he's got to be in control now, because he's been abused for so long since he's been in [this city]. He's standing his ground now and he's not taking no shit from anybody. The suspension made him worse.

Stressed and unhappy family members are left to deal with the emotional, social, medical and financial problems, which result from exclusion.

Future Prospects for Excluded Children

Pearce and Hillman argue (1998) that 65 per cent of compulsory school age children receiving court sentences were found to be either persistent truants or excluded pupils (Audit Commission 1996), whilst Graham and Bowling (1995) revealed a strong association between exclusion and offending. Exclusion has long-term effects in that it seriously disrupts educational careers, adds to the feeling of educational rejection, leads to under-achievement and contributes to wider social problems. The drive towards an information society leaves behind those who are poorly qualified, who are vulnerable to a life of social exclusion and marginalization. Permanently excluded young people of secondary school age were also frequently found to have committed offences in the year prior to exclusion or the year after it (in misspent youth no.93). There is therefore particular cause for concern with regard to children who experience long-tem permanent exclusion, as they may remain unsupervised for significant periods of time and are clearly at risk of descending into criminal activity.

Out of the 11 young people featured in this chapter, three were excluded (two permanently) for a criminal offence. Paul, who experienced multiple exclusions from both primary and secondary school, was excluded for being in the school office where it was assumed he had attempted to steal school property. Paul maintained his innocence but had also begun to develop a criminal history outside school which influenced the decision made to exclude. One excludee committed crimes only outside school, whereas two of the three aforementioned who had been excluded for criminal activity, never took up such activity outside school, and had not repeated their behaviours within school.

The parents in the study were very clear about the short- and long-term effects of exclusion on their children. They were concerned that their children should return to education as soon as possible, arguing that the lost education would have long-term detrimental effects on their child's opportunities. The Audit Commission argues that tackling truancy and exclusion is one way of helping reduce vulnerability to offending behaviour. The parents were aware that the socially disadvantaged position currently occupied by Black people would be compounded for their children, should they fail to achieve adequate qualifications. Whilst they may not be conversant with academic research on the matter, they made effective use of their own experiences and community knowledge about the short- and long-term effects of educational disadvantage on Black people. Certainly research suggests that people who leave school with little or no qualifications have poor prospects, with 'educational attainment at 16, the most important predictor of future participation in learning and of labour market prospects' (Pearce and Hillman 1998: 7). Indeed despite the major changes in policies and practices, the rate of children leaving school without any GCSE qualifications has stubbornly remained at 1 in 12, and of those, 75 per cent were not even entered for examinations. Evidence from the increased exclusion rates suggests that the practice of schools has moved away from inclusive education. Indeed exclusion from school, often accompanied by poor examination results, continues to be a powerful precursor to poverty, particularly in the form of underemployment and unemployment (Runnymede Trust 1995). Moreover the Black Report on health inequalities (1982), has shown that health risks coalesce around impoverishment, making poor people vulnerable to increased rates of morbidity and mortality.

Therefore the basic denial of an equal right to education which emanates from the experience of exclusion, can have implications which extend far beyond the sphere of schooling, affecting the 'extent to which people can make effective choices, engage in decision-making concerning their lives, contribute to the quality of life in their community and have a voice in collective decisions' (Blyth and Milner 1994: 30). In other words, Black children of today are at high risk of becoming tomorrow's socially excluded and the school plays a pivotal role in this process. Thus, in acknowledgement of the interconnectedness of risks, evidence-based literature now suggests that the focus of debate around and action on school exclusions should move away from envisaging it as essentially an educational matter (Blyth and Milner 1993, 1996).

At a community level having a large number of excluded Black young people will impact heavily on a relatively small ethnic group, leading to a large proportion of it being socially excluded and forced into poverty. Furthermore, high rates of school exclusion especially of Black boys, will consequently reduce the absolute number of potentially eligible men available to provide stability for future generations. This study clearly highlights the central role played by schooling in determining future health opportunities, employment prospects and social exclusion. Moreover the state is expected to pick up the escalating bill in the form of 'cost-shunting' and the provision of services such as compensatory education, second chance education, additional social services, extra burdens within the judicial system and long- and short-term health costs, especially those associated with lost opportunities and vulnerability to poverty (Parsons et al. 1997). Parents were keen that their children remain part of society and were conscious of the disproportionate number of African-Caribbean young people who were jobless, homeless, lacking in credentials and unable to make their way back into society. They were very well aware of the crucial role which exclusion plays in that process.

White Parents, Black Children

Two white parents participated in this study. Both were English women, born and brought up in the local area. One had a 14-year relationship with her 16-year-old son's father whereas the other had had a volatile relationship with her 15-year-old son's father which had culminated in domestic violence and the placing of her son in care for a short time. What is interesting about both mothers' testimonies is their consistency with those offered by the Black parents. Not only do they racialize their sons' experiences at school, but some of the reasons given for the continuation of problems are also the same.

One of the major problems faced by Philip, the son of Ms Short was the racial abuse and the school's lack of response to it. Philip attended a school in a predominantly white and working-class ward of the city. A demonstration had been held at the school by a support group of Black parents, and representatives from local community organizations because students had complained of racism from staff. The extent of the racism was exemplified in rumours of a petition, claimed to have been signed by many White members of staff at the school who felt that a large majority of the very small numbers of Black pupils at the school should be removed. When Philip retaliated to being called a Black bastard by another student; it was he who was seen as the perpetrator and subsequently punished. Nothing was done to his abuser.

'You've got one rule for one and another rule for another ... If it was my child who did something he would be out.'

(Ms Short, mother of Philip)

Another issue raised on several occasions was that of respect.

'If you want respect, you can't talk down to them [Black students]. You've got to talk to them as an equal, even though you are the teacher.'

(Ms Short, mother of Philip)

African-Caribbean young people have consistently argued for mutual respect between themselves and school staff (Runnymede 1995). This often provides the backdrop to a great deal of disgruntlement between young people and certain teachers. Kinder et al.'s (1996a) research revealed that the second most reported factor in pupils' disruptive behaviour was identified as the pupil:teacher relationship (see also OFSTED 1993), something also identified as important by parents (Kinder and Wilkin 1998). 'Having low expectations of pupils, treating them with a "lack of respect" (Keys and Fernandes 1993) or unfairly, led them to behave badly.'

'Teachers feel they can talk to you any way they want and that you're there for them not that they're there for you.'

(Mitchell, aged 16)

Ms Short considered the 'race' issue a vicious circle. Black young people were treated badly by White people and as a result she felt that they had developed a particular attitude to help them survive the racism. White people would respond to the attitudes which they encountered rather than considering their own contribution to the situation. She felt the place to break the circle was with a change in White people's own attitudes.

Ms Short stated that the disciplinary boundaries established by African-Caribbean parents were stricter than those set by their White counterparts and that she brought up her own children using the Black system which she considered to be a superior one.

'I'd kill my kids for this (unacceptable behaviour). White people don't pull up their kids the way that I would, or the way that you (Interviewer) would pull up your kids. I'd slap their face off, if they did it to me ... I haven't brought my kids up like that.'

(Ms Short, mother of Phillip)

Ms Short was aware that even in situations where her son's school had attempted to look seriously at issues of 'race', this work remained marginal, reflecting research which has highlighted the difficulties faced by staff attempting to support Black students in school (Runnymede 1998). She also felt that this work often took all responsibility away from schools to address particular issues themselves. A Black community worker had been brought into her son's school to resolve discipline issues involving African-Caribbean students.

> 'They brought Brenton (community worker) into the school so if a Black child got into trouble at school, he would have to deal with them. Brenton's Black. He'll know how to discipline those Black children. [I asked] "what do you mean Brenton knows how to deal with them?" [The Headteacher said] "We're not trained to deal with them" ... These aliens with Black skin and antennaes on their heads ... we're not trained to deal with them! ... It's like smashing your head against a brick wall ... Black kids just popped up, out of the sky, so she wasn't trained to deal with them.'

> (Ms Short, mother of Philip)

What appalled this parent most was the belief held by teachers within the school that Black children are so very difficult and different that until staff become specialized, there is nothing which teachers could do to support their needs. In the meantime it was customary (the organizational cultural approach) for Black pupils to remain either in educational limbo within the school walls or to be exiled beyond them through the process of exclusion.

Ms Short, like her Black counterparts, prioritized education and when she learned of her son's exclusion, visited the school, appealed against the result and sought help from various individuals and agencies. She also employed a solicitor to accompany her to various meetings. She was also very concerned about her son's vulnerability to crime and wider social exclusion through unemployment and underemployment. However, as a member of a support group for Black parents, her racial background created a few problems. She often felt left out of proceedings which she related to her racial background, but this did not prevent her from becoming intensely involved in pressures on the school to account for their racism.

Penny, the mother of Adam who had experienced two permanent exclusions, one from primary school and one from secondary school, felt that the staff at Adam's primary school had never been able to support and work with a Black child. She was increasingly bitter about a series of incidents which she felt had been related to Adam's racial background. Adam had been teased at school because of his weight and had often retaliated. His first exclusion had occurred as a result of a teacher whom she described as 'well over six foot four' claiming that Adam has assaulted him whilst at primary school. The process of appealing the decision took such a long time that Penny simply enrolled him in secondary school, but again she felt the exclusion occurred because of teacher fears around the size and presumed aggression of Black male pupils.

What these mothers revealed is the importance of envisaging Black students as people with needs, some of which can be met through sensitive and responsive pastoral care. They also indirectly referred to their own racial backgrounds in the statements made about members of teaching staff or the White peers of their children. In recognizing the failure to distribute sanctions equitably in others, they illustrated an acute awareness of the differences in experience between them as White mothers, and their mixed parentage children. The isolation felt by many of the Black parents interviewed when attempting to secure alternative education for their children was compounded to a certain extent by the racial background of Ms Short. The support group set up by parents of children who had been excluded from Philip's school was comprised of Black parents. Though Ms Short had joined the group to support her son, the hostility felt by Black parents towards staff and indeed other children at this particular school would occasionally be pointed in her direction. The exclusion of Black children from school is not an issue about a homogeneous group but about a group of individuals. In the same way, earlier chapters pointed out the gendered differentiation that is necessary both between pupils and staff which is also central to the debate. Where issues of racism between staff and pupils are integral to a child's exclusion, the mixed identity of the pupil may not only affect how he/she responds to the situation but also the extent to which the child seeks help from the parent or the parent feels adequately equipped to support. These are important issues requiring further research and debate.

A Return to the Social Analysis of Racism, Personal and Institutional

Researchers and commentators on 'race' in the school setting have been keen to move towards a more complex understanding of the notion of racism and to explore the ways in which even the most committed anti-racist teachers may contribute to the racist outcomes which Black pupils endure (Macdonald et al. 1989). In the light of the MacPherson Report of the investigation of the death of Stephen Lawrence, attention has been turned to the issue of institutional racism.

> '. . . the collective failure of an organization to provide an appropriate and professional service to people because of their colour, culture or ethnic origin. It can be seen or detected in processes, attitudes and behaviour which amounts to discrimination through unwitting prejudice, ignorance, thoughtlessness and racist stereotyping which disadvantages minority ethnic people.'
>
> (MacPherson Report 1999 cited in *Guardian* 24/2/99 p. 5)

The government is likely to utilize the findings of the Report to extend the Race Relations Act and to focus on the issue of racism in its public sector agencies, which until now have not had the same degree of focus placed upon them as the private sector. Schools have been targeted for change and in the light of the evidence from this study there is much to be accomplished before schools become inclusive learning environments. Unfortunately, there is much evidence which suggests that the opposite is happening and that many African-Caribbean children somehow are expected to learn in one of the most racially hostile atmospheres to be encountered in Britain. Parents and their children attest to the use of the following words by white children, in their quest for playground power, 'Black bastard', 'Black cunt', 'Nigger', 'Paki', 'Wog'. No excuse is made for the repetition of these words within the text because it is important that the rawness of this language is not lost and that the impact that it has on its recipients can be properly judged. Fights both verbal and physical occur between Black and White students as a result of racist abuse and if such behaviour were to occur in the delivery of other services, such as housing, or in the workplace, the victims would have recourse to the law. Industrial tribunals all over the country try such cases on a daily basis, but this does not occur when vulnerable young people are compulsorily sent for some eleven years, three terms a year, between 9 am and 3.30 pm to an establishment known as school. Racial abuse and threats of violence are for many the daily reality of the school playground and it is to that battleground that African-Caribbean children are being sent and told to learn. These detrimental conditions are then too often supported by teachers, who may refuse or feel unable to respond to the needs of their Black pupils because the procedures for dealing with racist abusers remains untested. Whilst the leadership fails to provide overt support for dealing adequately with the problem, nothing will change. Black students and boys in particular will rebel. They will take on the fight themselves and in so doing will continue to be envisaged as the perpetrators rather than the victims and they will continue to be excluded. Teachers may well be unaware of how their own unwitting behaviour contributes to this process and of how the assumptions they have about the African-Caribbean culture and its people may lead to confrontation. However, changes in the law will no longer allow this unwitting institutionally racist behaviour to go unchallenged. Despite evidence that schools as institutions fail Black children, a spokeswoman for the National Union of Teachers contested the definition of institutional racism as applied to education.

A spokeswoman for the NUT said it was 'extraordinarily unfair' to condemn the whole system. 'The teaching profession has done more than any other institution to counter racism. It is time that we need to see a greater representation of ethnic minorities on the staff, but this doesn't represent racism.'

(*Guardian* 24/2/99 p. 5)

The parents and students in this study have made it quite clear that in African-Caribbean culture, equality cannot and will not be separated from respect. This requires teachers to speak with and deal with them as students and parents in a fair and just manner. The mere existence of such differential exclusion rates across the country indicates that this simply is not happening.

Conclusion

When a Black child experiences an exclusion from school, both the rights of the child and the parent become problematized. Much of the construction of educational rights for excluded pupils and their parents, is inextricably linked with policy and the relinquishing of schools to market forces. It has been shown that the competitiveness which emanates from the current educational climate can prove detrimental to the rights of children generally (Jeffs 1995; Whitney 1993; Newell 1991; Osler 1994), but where these experiences of rights-negation are compounded by race and exclusion, they begin to impinge negatively upon the parental rights so often lauded as particularly well catered for within educational policy. The discrepancy between official and parental discourses of the constitution of rights within education is quite clearly articulated by the parents of Black excluded children and it is this, together with disproportionate exclusions of Black children, and recent research highlighting the increasing underachievement of African-Caribbean pupils (Gillborn and Gipps 1996), which constructs racialized groups as marginal within the education system.

Black children and their families have been failed by government decisions to apply the rigours of industry and the use of managerialism to the complexity of needs inherent within the school setting. The translation of market forces into human services, without regard to the needs of the most vulnerable was inevitably going to lead to a widening of the resource gap between the haves and the have-nots. The rise in bureaucracy, the change in requirements, the new policies and developments, have contributed to the high exclusion rates of African-Caribbean students. During times of upheaval, difficult problems may overwhelm the managers who may be tempted to resort to ready-made answers. Drawing from the statements made by the contributors to this study and the definition offered by the MacPherson Report (1999), individual and institutional racism clearly exists within schools.

Changes are undoubtedly needed at an institutional, LEA and national level in order to reduce the high rates of African-Caribbean exclusion. Adaptive organizational cultures must be developed that will need headteachers who care deeply about social justice, their 'customers' (pupils and parents) 'stockholders' (the local community) and employees. They will need to support this through the use of processes and the utilization of people's skills, to create change up and down the organizational structure. Such an approach, particularly in light of the findings of the 1999

MacPherson Report will require public service-based management styles, which should serve the interests of the groups identified above. The leader, or in this case the headteacher, becomes crucial to ensuring the possibility of successful change. Research needs to address the influence of managerialism on the ability to be adaptive within the school setting. Thus combating inequality and injustice relies on the dissemination of good practice, particularly from 'leaders', which lamentably contradicts managerialism's stress upon dissecting work into planning and doing. Similarly, government needs to reflect upon its own role in supporting the rise and continuation of school managerialism and identify ways in which it can contribute to an actual decline in exclusion both formal and informal, focusing attention on the needs of those most vulnerable to the problem to ensure that they establish requirements from LEAs and schools which will effect real change. Society is judged by how it treats its weakest members. It is time that the voices of vulnerable parents and pupils are given priority in making the service of education both accountable and accessible to its users. The school exclusion of Black children within the context of parental exclusion from areas of employment, housing and services, does little to provide a safe and enviable future for young people. School exclusion must be seen as more than an educational issue. It is the bridge between the individual and future opportunity, it can offer the chance of life within the professional classes or it can move us towards the dead-end of social exclusion. Without a concerted effort, Britain will follow in the footsteps of America, creating ghettos of unemployed, unemployable unqualified, socially excluded Black communities.

In the absence of a concerted effort against individual and institutional racism, it is unlikely that any of the huge number of papers, guidelines, recommendations and reports on how to combat general and specific forms of exclusion will be put into practice and/or made effective. Practical and financial support must be made available to keep Black pupils in school and make schools a place where all pupils have equal access to learning. Excluding disproportionate numbers of Black pupils is indicative of a problem unresolved and must not be taken as a problem solved.

7 Future Prospects – Towards Inclusive Education for All

Introduction

The preceding chapters have explored the impact of race, class and gender on the interactions of pupils and teachers in the classroom setting and school in general. The research has sought to investigate the processes involved that help to explain the differential rates of school exclusion between pupils of different ethnic backgrounds, social class and gender. The research has focused on the often delicate balance between power and resistance.

The research undertaken has built on previous research findings on school exclusion and broadened it by examining how changing policies can affect the school processes which lead to exclusion. To provide an adequate explanation for differential rates of exclusion, school processes have then been explored in relation to the nature of interactions between schools, teachers and pupils. The book has also sought to disentangle how race, gender and class impact on these interactions. The after-effects of exclusion have also been discussed and how school exclusion can exacerbate a variety of forms of social exclusion. The research has also attempted to build on recent work on masculinity (Mac an Ghaill 1994; Sewell 1997) which is particularly important given the disproportionate number of males excluded. The research also suggests that the simplistic view of antagonistic relationships between pupils and teachers is in fact structured within the recent changes in educational policy.

The intention of this concluding chapter is to review the discussions developed in the preceding chapters and by so doing look at ways in which the negative social consequences of school exclusion can be avoided. This involves the formulation of recommendations and initiatives based on the experiences of pupils and teachers discussed in the previous chapters. Initiatives relate to in-school interventions as well as wider policy interventions. The findings and recommendations of the MacPherson Report (1999) will also be addressed, in so far as they relate to schooling, education and 'institutional racism'.

Changing Policy Considerations

At the outset of this book it was indicated that the relationship between exclusion and race can be situated within the wider context of educational policy and the need for schools to have 'desirable' pupils in order to enhance or maintain their status. This is particularly significant when considering the rapid increase in school exclusions over recent years.

The increased marketization of education and the resulting publication of league tables of school performance has made it apparent that, in order for positions to be maintained, schools treat some pupils as more desirable than others. Where it operates, parental choice primarily enables parents to avoid schools with substantial numbers of pupils who are different from themselves. Indeed, it is difficult to separate the effect of the ERA from the increasing number of school exclusions, especially of African-Caribbean males. The issue is not just one of parents choosing schools but of schools choosing pupils, thereby redefining their population. Thus in practice, through a variety of entrance measures and selection procedures, it is frequently the case that it is the school choosing the pupils rather than vice versa.

It is possible to regard exclusion as one of the ways in which schools choose pupils. The large increase in the rate of school exclusions in recent years may be part of the process whereby schools are selecting and deselecting pupils. For schools, the marketability and desirability of pupils operates through social class, race and gender. Not all groups are equally desirable in terms of their potential impact on school 'performance' and league table position. Within a context that has become increasingly consumerist and competitive it is not surprising to find that the school processes of pupil selection and deselection have a disproportionately adverse effect on some groups of pupils. The marketability of pupils may be related to their ability to give the school the qualities it is looking for.

One effect of the ERA has been to encourage the media, government and OFSTED to concentrate on the overall performance of schools, as evidenced through measures of performance in national tests and examinations. This focus leads to the neglect of what schools are doing for individual pupils or disadvantaged groups of pupils. Teachers face increasing pressure to produce a performance for a class group or subject that is easily measured. They therefore have less time to spend with individual pupils who may exhibit behavioural or learning difficulties. The pressure and stress on teachers to produce a measurable performance is not compatible with meeting the needs of all groups of children equally.

The 1998 School Standards and Framework Act has a focus on school exclusion, but it is still essentially blind to the differentials of race and class as they impact on school exclusions. The importance of racial stereotypes held by those working in schools and selecting/deselecting pupils is not addressed in recent education policies. It has been left to a government-sponsored report, the MacPherson Report (1999), which is not specifically concerned with education, to focus on racial stereotypes that are held throughout public institutions.

In addition to processes emanating from outside the school and impinging on school procedures and practices, there are other processes internal to the school. It is these internal procedures and practices that are determining the disproportionately high percentage of pupils of African-Caribbean origin who are being excluded from school. At the heart of this is the long recognized observation that relations between White teachers and Black pupils are far too often characterized by conflict. Bound up with this is the perception of Black pupils' attitudes towards authority. In addition, there is the contestation and resistance by Black pupils to teacher authority and their perception of their treatment by teachers. This has resonances with accounts of how schools treat their working-class pupils (Willis, 1977).

Black pupils, to an increasing extent, do not fit the concept of the 'ideal pupil'. This is with respect to both their marketization/desirability and their perceived reaction to authority, especially school authority. It is through both internal school practices and external policies that some groups of pupils become increasingly regarded as potential liabilities.

Empirical Implications

The empirical work undertaken as part of this investigation has revealed the way in which exclusion largely results from the nature of the relationship between schools and their pupils. These relationships are often bound up with the nature of the schools' response to the issue of discipline. Schools vary in their exclusion policies and practices. School policies were found to vary from what might be termed 'zero tolerance', which involved a relatively quick recourse to fixed-term exclusion, to policies where there were either no clear guidelines or sanctions were simply left to the discretion of individual members of staff. This range of policies resulted in varying exclusion rates and different attitudes by schools towards the use of exclusion. Therefore, pupils at different schools varied in their likelihood of experiencing sanctions.

Schools had a variety of types of ethos and these were expressed through the views of headteachers and senior staff, particularly in relation to their 'disruptive minorities'. Sanctions were seen to be needed in order to reinforce the type of behaviour the schools found acceptable and as the means of reinforcing teacher/school authority. Where schools were adamant as to the importance of the latter, there tended to be higher rates of exclusion, especially where headteachers and senior staff regarded the use of exclusion as inevitable, and regretted the loss of physical punishment as a sanction. Discipline was found to relate to ideas about punishment, with the assumption that this would have a positive outcome for pupils. Schools frequently emphasized the division between the well-behaved majority and the poorly-behaved minority. This division was often perceived by teachers, senior staff and headteachers and created a climate of conflict between staff and pupils.

The conflict that occurs between pupils and schools has a relationship with the extent to which schools resort to sanctions as a response to pupil resistance. When the conflict involves African-Caribbean and Asian pupils, it is important to examine the nature of the conflict in relation to the resistance these groups are exhibiting and the extent to which this derives from their racialized positions. Most Black people are aware of the value of education. What is being resisted and contested is the nature of the power and control expressed by the schools. This is coupled with the extent to which pupils feel or experience discrimination and how this permeates through to the way in which teachers perceive their behaviour. Black pupils are contesting and resisting the nature of the knowledge the school is reproducing and the nature of the authority and power used by the schools.

The nature of the school ethos was found to be important in the extent to which pupils' responses and behaviour could be regarded as resistant. Resistances were also found to vary with the extent to which pupils perceived sanction policies as fair and/or their ability to get staff to listen to them. It was also clear that the extent to which pupils considered treament to be fair was influenced by their perception as to whether incidents with and attitudes of teachers, were racist. Where Black pupils perceived White pupils as misbehaving without experiencing sanctions, they would place their strategies of resistance within a racial context. Variations in experiences of exclusion by pupils were perceived as indicative of racism. When teachers were unwilling to address accusations of racism levelled at them by pupils, conflict was often exacerbated. However, suggestions in the March 1999 OFSTED report of institutional racism in schools, have been met with denials by teachers and their unions.

Pupils resisted teacher control in a variety of ways. Although teachers often recognized the nature of this and the reasons behind it, they varied in their attitudes to addressing it. Pupil 'disaffection' was clearly identified as a background factor, but some teachers felt powerless in assisting pupils. This was particularly evident when they disagreed with the sanction policies of senior staff.

Pupil resistance to schooling and school processes and their responses to the use of sanctions, was found not merely to be a matter of school policy and ethos, but how the practice of these was mediated through the racialized and gendered positions of the pupils. The schools in the study had a variety of complex ways in which they were involved in the production of masculinities and femininities. The disproportionate involvement of Black males in exclusion has been known for some time and there is an interrelating of race and gender involved in this outcome. It is important to know how schools perceive and respond to black masculinity. However, it is also important to include Black femininities here, as young Black women also perceive and experience the influence of race in their response to school sanctions.

The research has examined how masculinity, femininity and 'race' intersect to produce complex responses to school sanctions. It is Black pupil masculinity that has received the greatest attention in theorizing. The research here shows how schools and teachers can produce attitudes that lead to the perception of Black male pupils as being more aggressive. In a response to this, some teachers wish to (re-)gain control through more physical means. In fact to make control become more heavily masculine. Teachers were more likely to see Black male pupils as a threat. This involved an attendant disproportionate involvement of those pupils in school sanctions.

Teacher perception of pupils' behaviour could also lead to Black male pupils finding themselves placed in lower sets and pupil referral units. Exclusion from higher status academic knowledge could in turn lead to Black masculinity being defined in terms of sporting prowess. However, this was not always the case. Black male pupils respond in complex ways to their perception of teacher attitudes. This may involve both conforming to dominant stereotypes and a rejection of them.

In terms of the experience of school sanctions, there is no equality of outcome when similar behaviours by White/Black female and male pupils involve different experiences. Black males have been known for some time to be disproportionately involved in school exclusions.

It is also important to analyse whether male and female pupils respond to sanctions differently and how any differences are related to the ways in which schooling produces definitions of masculinity and femininity. For many African-Caribbean male pupils, schooling involves confrontation to the consequent neglect of a focus on academic achievement. Black female pupils were also seen to be involved in confrontation, but the academic outcome for them is generally more positive. However, these pupils don't respond to the threat of school sanctions in a clearly identical way.

This study found that few Black females saw differences between themselves and their male peers in how they responded to school sanctions. Indeed, male pupils often did respond to the power of teachers in ways not specifically defined as masculine. The gendered background of teachers was also shown to be important in how different definitions of pupils are produced. Male teachers appeared more likely to use stereotypical notions of masculinity to exert influence and control over male pupils.

Black females are known to assert that their ethnicity is of greater importance than their gender in its effect on their economic and social positions. Indeed, Black female pupils were found to be responded to by teachers in similar ways to Black male pupils. The response of these pupils to sanctions and exclusion was partially mediated through gendered positions. Many pupils, irrespective of racial background, attempted to resist teacher power. African-Caribbean and Asian pupils were also seen to do this, but it was mediated through concerns related to gender and racial background. Black female pupils were seen to be more likely to stress their lack of power and this may be related to their feelings of helplessness in the face of teacher authority.

The greatest differentials in the ways in which pupils adapted and responded to school were based on 'race'. Teachers did sometimes consider Black male pupils to pose more discipline problems and this is related to images of Black males. However, it is race that is the dominant dimension in this process. Teachers tend to regard African-Caribbean pupils as an homogeneous group, which is more likely to be disruptive, whereas White pupils were likely to be heterogenized.

The nature of teacher perception of Black pupils is part of the process involved in creating high rates of exclusion. However, schools do exclude pupils at different rates. Therefore schools do have an effect on exclusion rates and this can be related to their 'ethos'. This ethos is developed under a range of complex influences. On the one hand, internal policies, structures and attitudes of senior staff are involved. On the other, there is also a range of external pressures and factors. The latter have, in recent years, appeared primarily as competition between schools, and performance as indicated in school league tables. As a result, schools pay greater attention to improving performance, as shown on measured outcomes and less attention to the needs of the disaffected. This change has been accompanied by the spreading culture of managerialism in schools. Managerialism results in an emphasis on such factors as economy and efficiency, which in the school setting means a greater stress on indicators such as examination results and less stress on trying to meet the needs of less motivated pupils. The high rates of exclusion of African-Caribbean pupils should be placed within this climate of change.

Superimposed on a culture which emphasizes the importance of measurable performance indicators, is the way in which some schools exhibit a lack of sensitivity and understanding in meeting the needs of African-Caribbean children. Hence Black pupils and their parents often feel as though White children are treated more favourably. This does, however, vary by school. Schools with policies applied coherently and consistently are more successful in dealing with disruptive behaviour. Less effective schools have practices that are less supportive. Such schools tend to blame the pupils, with the implication that exclusion is meeting the needs of the school. Even in schools with clear policies, the practice was often seen by Black pupils and parents as divisive. This was particularly evident in how they saw disciplinary practices as disadvantaging Black children. Practices that aim at resolving conflict, rather than stressing harmony, may be the more successful and less discriminating in outcome. Where there is an inability to solve problems and little commitment to equality, exclusion rates are higher.

As noted earlier, changes brought about by the ERA have resulted in less tolerance towards aberrant student behaviour, with the increasing probability of exclusion being used to solve the problem. Black parents and students still see too many teachers ignoring racist behaviour and being less than sensitive to the needs of ethnic minority pupils. If Black pupils see that teachers are not addressing their needs and not dealing with the racism they experience, it creates a climate where disobedience occurs. Disobedience is the main reason leading to exclusion. Therefore, it happens that Black pupils are sometimes excluded for reacting to the racism they experience.

When Black pupils perceive or feel that teachers have low expectations of them, or are treating them unequally, they are more likely to express their reaction through aberrant behaviour. Black students frequently felt that in being excluded they were treated unfairly by schools. One consequence of unequal and unfair treatment by White teachers is that pupils and parents emphasize the need for Black teachers. This is because the White teachers involved lack the necessary sophistication to understand the effects of racism on students. One indication of this is that when Black pupils confront racism in school they are often seen by teachers as having behavioural problems.

African-Caribbean parents place great importance on academic success and achievement through education. It is in this context that we explain the strong feelings of Black parents and children when exclusion happens, particularly as they know that it is likely to have a lasting effect on the pupil. This also makes them more suspicious of teachers. Despite this, the parents of excludees want their children to return to schooling as soon as possible. This is seen as particularly important, given that excludees are at a much greater risk of longer-term social exclusion.

A constantly recurring theme for Black parents and pupils is how Black students, especially boys, should confront racism and racist abusers, when in the process they are likely to be seen by teachers as the perpetrators of problems and so risk exclusion. Also frequently stressed is how teacher assumptions about Black people may lead to confrontation. They do not feel that teachers deal with them fairly. The high rate of exclusion is seen as testament to this.

This study has examined the complex interaction of teacher–pupil relations, teacher perceptions and expectations and superimposed on these, structural processes operating at the policy level. It is this complex interaction that leads to the differential experience of school sanctions by African-Caribbean pupils as compared with other pupil groups. It can be argued that what is at work here and is leading to disproportionately high rates of exclusion is institutional racism (Sasson 1993). Sasson refers to anecdotal evidence that, 'when White youngsters are turned off schools and the curriculum, they truant. Black youngsters are forced by their parents to go to school where they become disruptive and in due course expelled' (p. 11). However, when this disruptive behaviour is exhibited, Black pupils still have a different experience of school sanctions than other groups. When Black pupils experience racism in school from whatever source, they react. However, it appears that their reaction is regarded as the problem, rather than the racism they have experienced. The unfairness that Black pupils identify refers to the fact that they see sanctions being applied more stringently to their reaction to racism than they see them being applied to the racism itself.

Converging Views: Runnymede (1998), MacPherson (1999) and OFSTED (1999)

Recently, the Chairman of the CRE has commented on the low priority given to combating racism in schools and three recent reports have highlighted this problem: Runnymede (1998), MacPherson (1999) and OFSTED (1999).

The Runnymede Trust Report (1998)

The first of these reports stems from research undertaken by the Runnymede Trust and is focused on the general problem of raising the achievement of African-Caribbean pupils. Central to this problem is the need to address the high rate of exclusion. The two, however, are regarded as inseparable and hence the report recommends what it refers to as a 'whole school approach'. The report stresses a no-blame approach in that teachers and others need to work together in a variety of community initiatives. Teachers need to know that they are not being singled out for blame or criticism as they are intricately and vitally involved in solutions to the problem of dispro-portionate exclusion rates. Genuine partnerships need to be developed, but the report emphasizes that, currently, these are rare.

It is in this context that the report recommends collaboration and dialogue between schools, community, parents and pupils as the key to raising African-Caribbean pupil achievement. Initiatives must target those pupils at risk from exclusion and focus on raising motivation, self-esteem and teacher expectation. Having more Black teachers and mentors is seen as important in this. The report goes on to recommend a large number of initiatives and measures to reduce exclusion and raise achievement. The difficulties that Black pupils have at school should be addressed in a specific and targeted way. Initiatives should therefore avoid being 'colour blind' and instead must target pupils most at risk of exclusion.

Measures must have the support of senior staff to prevent the issue of school exclusion being seen as marginal. Headteacher commitment is also vital. It is important that a positive school ethos is created, in which teachers listen to and respect pupils, and in which teachers are given support to reach each target relating to achievement and exclusion. In this respect, initiatives to reduce exclusion must incorporate the views of those pupils who have been excluded as to how they think exclusions could be reduced. Targets should be set within schools in relation to the behaviour management of pupils and involve subject staff. Targets for behaviour must also be closely tied to academic achievement.

In relation to pupils at risk of exclusion or having been excluded, the report suggests that support for these pupils should be integrated, with the aim of raising pupil motivation and achievement. Pupils excluded should be given home-based work to undertake to reduce problems of falling behind.

Schools should establish conflict resolution techniques for pupils. Teachers need to examine the underlying causes of disputes between pupils, and between themselves and pupils, rather than only concentrating on the immediate effects of confrontation. Teachers also need to recognize that racist name calling and abuse are real problems. There must also be an agreed procedure for dealing with racist incidents, as it is these that can lead to Black pupils reacting in ways that result in sanctions being applied to them. Important in this is that teachers must be consistent in allocating sanctions and with giving praise.

In relation to the whole school approach suggested by the report, schools are asked to consult with community groups, youth workers, parents and pupils. Initiatives to raise Black pupil achievement, recognizing that reducing the exclusion problem is part of this, should be integrated into schools' plans. At the national level the report goes on to suggest that the government should set national targets to reduce the number of African-Caribbean pupils excluded. In-service and initial teacher training should provide teachers with skills to address issues of teacher stereotyping and low expectations, particularly of African-Caribbean boys.

The MacPherson Report (1999)

A very large number of initiatives involving school and community are described and recommended by the Runnymede Report. These received national media attention. Receiving much greater media, national and government attention has been the publication of the MacPherson Report (1999), investigating the murder of Stephen Lawrence. This report did not have a specific remit on education or school exclusion, but related primarily to the handling of the investigation into the racist murder of Stephen Lawrence. However, the report produced a wide ranging set of recommendations not confined to the issue of policing. The report identified many issues to do with racism working in society at large. In this regard the report did suggest action that needed to be undertaken in schools and by the education system, in order to address racism. The report did indicate that some schools have resisted anti-racist policies, and even where they do exist these policies are largely ineffective. There was a need identified to combat racism in pupils, in order to reduce racist incidents which affect the behaviour of black pupils.

The report produced a number of recommendations for schools in relation to combating racism. The one particular measure relating to school exclusions was that schools should publish data on exclusions broken down by ethnic group. There should also be a league table of pupils excluded. A number of other measures were recommended that have a bearing on school exclusion, including that schools should record all racist incidents and report them to pupils' parents, governors and the LEA. The number of such incidents should be published annually by schools. The report identified it as important that the national curriculum be amended, by incorporating issues of preventing racism and valuing cultural diversity. Hence, the national curriculum should reflect a diverse multi-ethnic society. The necessity to teach anti-racism as part of the national curriculum was also recommended. Racial awareness should also be provided in the classroom.

The OFSTED Report (1999)

Following soon after the MacPherson Report has been the OFSTED Report: Raising the Attainment of Ethnic Minority Pupils (1999). The focus of this report is the performance of ethnic minority pupils in schools. It examines the strategies that schools use and could use, to raise attainment, along with policies for tackling stereotyping and ensuring high expectations. All of these are vital ingredients in tackling the problem of school exclusion among African-Caribbean pupils. The report finds that this group of pupils 'make a sound start in primary schools but their performance shows a marked decline at secondary level'. This suggests that the major problems are at this level.

The report finds limited evidence of schools having positive strategies to address the problems faced by African-Caribbean pupils. Few schools monitor initiatives to raise attainment or have clear procedures for monitoring the implementation of Equal Opportunity policies. There is limited use of ethnic monitoring in schools and few schools review their curriculum and pastoral strategies to ensure that they are sensitive to ethnic minority pupils. In those schools which have been successful in raising the attainment of ethnic minority pupils, senior managers make it clear that underperformance is not acceptable and they challenge staff to make it clear what they intend to do about it. Schools in which ethnic minority pupils do well, understand the 'hostility' the pupils face. These schools develop successful strategies for countering stereotyping and this can have a positive effect on confidence and self-esteem. Schools with successful race relations have an ethos where pupils can express their concerns and play a part in their resolution.

In relation to exclusion, few schools analyse data by ethnicity or consider the causes of exclusion. Some schools have discovered that African-Caribbean pupils involved in fights and confrontation had experienced racist abuse prior to the incidents. 'Those minority ethnic pupils who react angrily to racist insults often find themselves at the sharp end of sanctions. Schools must make it explicit that racist behaviour is wrong and will not be tolerated' (OFSTED 1999: 38). The research undertaken in the present study has emphasized the role of unfairness in the perception of the lives of Black pupils. Approaches and strategies to deal with this are vital in tackling the problem of excessive school exclusions of these pupils.

The OFSTED Report echoes the Runnymede Report in that it emphasizes whole school policies. It stresses that schools should monitor pupil achievement, behaviour, attendance and exclusion by ethnic group and use this data to set targets for improvement. Schools must counter harassment and stereotyping by having policies that are clear and with practical guidance on how to deal with racist behaviour. An open school ethos is part and parcel of this. LEAs need to set targets to reduce the exclusions of African-Caribbean pupils and should also collect and collate data on exclusion and behaviour by ethnic group.

Conclusion

These three reports resonate clearly with the investigations and findings discussed in the previous chapters. The emphasis must involve a change of school culture from exclusion to inclusion. It must be remembered that school exclusion infringes the rights of children to education. Those pupils who are excluded often find it difficult to regain entry to formal education. When faced with exclusion, parents must have the ability to exercise their right to places for their children in other schools. The increased marketization of schooling and competition between schools is leading to a situation where exclusion is more and not less likely. Rather than seeing exclusion as a means of solving problems, schools need to adopt approaches that aim at keeping and retaining pupils they may perceive as less desirable. They need to move to a position where they regard all pupils as potential high achievers.

It is not sufficient simply to eschew overt acts or words of racism. We have to recognize that Black pupils are not expected to do as well as White students and/or are expected to be louder or less well-behaved than White children. It is possible to improve pupils' achievements by treating them as if they will succeed or behave well. So, if others are treated as if they will perform badly or fail, we must bear responsibility for this. Pupils can live down to the schools expectations of them. Strategies and an ethos must be put in place, whereby Black students have high self-esteem if they are to do themselves justice. Others' perceptions of Black pupils can be changed, along with their own perceptions of themselves.

These perceptions are inextricably linked to the over-representation of African-Caribbean pupils in school exclusion statistics. This problem has to be tackled in conjunction with an overall school policy of raising achievement. As such a whole school approach is vital and should incorporate a large number of interconnected measures. Headteachers must take a strong lead on equal opportunities. If necessary, appropriate further training may be required. Both in-service and initial teacher training have to incorporate anti-racism training and all that it involves, in relation to teacher expectations and stereotypes. Black pupils frequently stress the importance of having Black teachers in their schools. Black mentor programmes are also known to assist in increasing self-esteem and raising pupils' expectations of themselves. Underpinning the success of such programmes is the building of strong links between schools and the communities they serve.

It is impossible to measure improvements without monitoring. It is vital for schools to monitor achievement, exclusion and behaviour incidents by ethnic group. Accompanying this monitoring must be the setting of targets with all school staff involved, together with a clear commitment from senior staff to improvement. Target setting is inseparable from having a clear strategy for preventing exclusion. Part and parcel of a clear strategy is to listen to and learn from both pupils and parents. There must be incorporated in this strategy clear targeting and tracking of pupil achievement and behaviour by ethnic group.

Schools and teachers must be seen to be intolerant of racism. Every school must have a clear procedure for responding to racist incidents and treat them as a potential source of poor behaviour, rather than responding to pupils' behaviour which is itself the reaction to racism. Schools have to investigate grievances and be vigilant in those relating to racism. Strategies for dealing with stereotyping need to be linked to the role of developing a curriculum that is truly multi-cultural and anti-racist.

It is not simply a matter of policies for schools. A lead needs to be taken by LEAs and government. In this respect the present government has already given its response to the MacPherson Report (1999). Schools will be required to log all racist incidents and report patterns and the frequency of racism to the LEA. Parents have the right to know what action schools will take to tackle racism. The government has also stated that it agrees with the MacPherson Report call to include anti-racism in the national curriculum. However, it believes that the national curriculum already addresses the diverse nature of British society and schools will not have to publish league tables of racist behaviour as recommended in the report. Rather, the government believes that this would penalize those schools which are open and honest about racism. However, as noted in the OFSTED Report (1999), such schools are relatively rare.

Concluding Implications

So, what implications should finally be drawn from this study? First, we must acknowledge the importance placed on education by African-Caribbean parents and their children. Because of this, many disaffected Black pupils remain in school and want to be educated, instead of which they frequently end up excluded. Their disaffected White peers more often simply stay away from school and, thus, are no longer seen as a problem.

As well as wanting to be educated, indeed in order to be educated, Black pupils need to have the differentiated recognition and respect that their White peers attract. Colour blind treatment is unacceptable. Pupils need racially aware teachers, who interact with them taking account of their colour and culture and who encourage diversity, not unthinking conformity. Likewise, class and gender cannot be ignored.

Treating any group of pupils as if they are homogeneous is a mistake; and treating all Black pupils alike, without reference to their class, gender or other individual characteristics, is both racist and insulting. White pupils are far more likely to be treated in a differentiated way. We also have to accept that schools that are run on competitive lines, sensitive to the market in which they operate and their position in the performance league tables, are likely to succumb to a managerialist culture. In turn, this will further marginalize or even ignore the needs of disaffected pupils, rather than provide the positive and supportive ethos that they require. In such a culture teachers are more likely to ignore racism and thereby further alienate and incite their black pupils. They will certainly lose respect and encounter a lack of co-operation. But when those same Black pupils refuse to accept racism and instead react to it, their behaviour may very well be seen as the problem. Punishing understandable responses to racism, whilst ignoring the racism itself, is hardly the way to engage Black pupils in the education enterprise. Black people, whether parents or pupils, are not going to ignore racism. Having already fought and overcome slavery and segregation, exclusion from school is not going to be accepted without complaint, where it is imposed for reacting to racist taunts, slurs, insults or other racist behaviour. Schools and their communities have to recognize the inter-connectedness of race, class, gender and power and then act together to ensure that cultural diversity is both respected and valued. Exclusion from school has to be recognized as indicative of a problem yet to be solved, not as one that has been resolved.

References

Aggleton, P. (1987) *Rebels Without a Cause: Middle-class Youth and the Transition from School to Work*, London: Falmer Press.

Alexander, C. (1996) *The Art of Being Black: The Creation of Black British Youth Identities*, Oxford: Clarendon Press.

Allen, T. (1994) 'The exclusion of pupils from school: the need for reform', *Journal of Social Welfare and Family Law*, 2: 145–62.

Alvesson, M. (1987) *Organisation, Theory and Technocratic Consciousness: Rationality, Ideology and Quality of Work*, Aldershot: De Gruyter.

Anyon, J. (1983) 'Intersections of gender and class: accommodation and resistance by working class and affluent females to contradictory sex-role ideologies', in S. Walker and L. Burton (eds) *Gender, Class and Education*, Lewes: Falmer Press.

Askew, S. and Ross, C. (1988) *Boys Don't Cry: Boys and Sexism in Education*, Milton Keynes: Open University Press.

Audit Commission (1996) *Misspent Youth ... Young People and Crime*, London: HMSO.

Back, L. (1996) *New Ethnicities and Urban Culture: Racisms and Multiculture in Young Lives*, London: UCL Press.

Bash, L. (1989) 'Education goes to market' in L. Bash and D. Coulby (eds) *The Education Reform Act: Competition and Control*, London: Cassell.

Bennathan, M. (1992) 'The care and education of troubled children', *Young Minds Newsletter*, 10, March.

Benson, C. (1996) 'Resisting the trend to exclude' in E. Blyth and J. Milner (eds) *Exclusion from School: Inter-professional Issues for Policy and Practice*, London: Routledge.

Benyon, J. and Solomos, J. (eds) (1987) *The Roots of Urban Unrest*, Oxford: Pergamon Press.

Blair, M. (1994) 'Interviews with black families' in R. Cohen et al. *Schools Out: The Family Perspective on School Exclusion*, London: Barnardo's and Family Service Units.

Blyth, E. and Milner, J. (1993) 'Exclusion from school: a first step in exclusion from society?', *Children and Society*, 13(1).

Blyth, E. and Milner, J. (1994) 'Exclusion from school and victim-blaming', *Oxford Review of Education*, 20(3).

Blyth, E. and Milner, J. (1996) *Exclusion from School: Inter-professional Issues for Policy and Practice*, London: Routledge.

References

Bourdieu, P. (1987) 'What makes a social class? On the theoretical and practical existence of groups', *Berkeley Journal of Sociology*, 32: 1–18.

Bourdieu, P. and Passeron, J. C. (1977) *Reproduction in Education, Society and Culture*, Beverley Hills: Sage.

Bourne, J., Bridges, L. and Searle, C. (1994) *Outcast England: How Schools Exclude Black Children*, London: Institute of Race Relations.

Bowles, S. and Gintis, H. (1976) *Schooling in Capitalist America*, London: Routledge & Kegan Paul.

Brah, A. (1992) 'Difference, diversity and differentiation' in J. Donald and A. Rattansi (eds) *'Race', Culture and Difference*, London: Sage Publications in association with the Open University.

Bridges, L. (1994) 'Exclusions: how did we get here?', in *Outcast England*, London: Institute of Race Relations.

Brittan, A. and Maynard, M. (1984) *Sexism, Racism and Oppression*, Oxford: Basil Blackwell.

Bryan, B., Dadzie, S. and Scafe, S. (1985) *Heart of the Race*, London: Virago.

Callender, C. (1998) *Education For Empowerment*, Stoke-on-Trent: Trentham Books.

Campbell, D. (1995) 'Fury at Black crime claim: Howard supports "right to air issue"', *The Guardian*, 8 July.

Carlen, P. (1985) 'Out of care into custody' in P. Carlen and A. Worral (eds) *Gender, Crime and Justice*, Milton Keynes: Open University.

Cashmore, E. and Troyna, B. (eds) (1982) *Black Youth in Crisis*, London: Allen & Unwin.

Coard, B. (1971) *How the West Indian Child is made Educationally Sub-Normal in the British School System*, London: New Beacon Books.

Cohen, R. et al. (1994) *Schools Out: The Family Perspective on School Exclusion*, London: Barnardo's and Family Service Units.

Collins, P. (1990) *Black Feminist Thought*, New York: Routledge.

Connell, R. (1989) 'Cool guys, swots and wimps: the interplay of masculinity and education', *Oxford Review of Education*, 15: 291–303.

Connolly, P. (1994) 'Playing it by the rules: the politics of research' in *'Race' and Education* (British Educational Research Journal) 18(2).

Connolly, P. (1995) 'Racism, masculine peer-group relations and the schooling of African-Caribbean infant boys', *British Journal of Sociology of Education*, 16(1): 75–92.

CRE (Commission for Racial Equality) (1985) *Birmingham LEA and Schools: Referral and Suspension of Pupils*, London: CRE.

CRE (Commission for Racial Equality) (1996) *Exclusion From School: The Public Cost*, London: CRE.

Crozier, G. (1996) 'Black parents and school relationships: a case study', *Educational Review*, 48(3): 253–67.

Davies, L. (1983) 'Gender, resistance and power' in S. Walker and L. Barton (eds) *Gender, Class and Education*, Lewes: Falmer Press.

Davies, L. (1984) *Pupil Power: Deviance and Gender in School*, Lewes: Falmer Press.

de Pear, S. and Garner, P. (1996) 'Tales from the exclusion zone: the views of teachers and pupils' in E. Blyth and J. Milner (eds) *Exclusion from School: Inter-professional Issues for Policy and Practice*, London: Routledge.

DES (Department of Education and Science) (1989) 'Discipline in schools: report of the Committee of Inquiry chaired by Lord Elton', London: HMSO.

Devlin, A. (1995) *Criminal Classes: Offenders at School*, Winchester: Waterside Press.

DfE (Department of Education) (1992) *Exclusions: A Discussion Paper*, London: DfE.

DfE (Department of Education) (1994a) *Code of Practice on the Identification and Assessment of Special Educational Needs*, London: DfE.

DfE (Department of Education) (1994b) *Exclusions from School*, Circular No. 10/94, London: DfE.

DfE (Department of Education) (1995) *National Survey of Local Education Authorities' Policies and Procedures for the Identification of, and Provision for, Children who are out of School by Reason of Exclusion or Otherwise*, London, DfE.

DfEE (Department of Education and Employment) (1997) *Excellence in Schools*, Cm.3681, London: HMSO.

Docking, J.W. (1987) Control and Discipline in School: Perspectives and Approaches (2nd edn), London: Harper and Row.

Donald, J. and Rattansi, J. (eds), *'Race', Culture and Difference*, London: Sage.

Donovan, N. (ed.) (1998) *Second Chances: Exclusions from School and Equality of Opportunity*, London: New Policy Institute.

Dyson, M. (1993) *Reflecting Black: African American Cultural Criticism*, Minneapolis: University of Minnesota Press.

Ethnic Minorities Consultative Group (1994) *Exclusions Statistics 1993/4*, Nottingham LEA.

Farrington, D. and West, D. (1990) 'The Cambridge study in delinquent development: A long term follow-up of 411 London males' in H. Kerner and G. Kaiser (eds) *Criminality: Personality, Behaviour and Life History*, London: Springer Verlag.

Foster, P. (1990) *Policy and Practice in Multicultural and Anti-racist Education*, London: Routledge.

Foster, P. (1991) 'Case still not proven: a reply to Cecile Wright', *British Educational Research Journal*, 12(2): 165–70.

Foster, P., Gomm, R. and Hammersley, M. (1996) *Constructing Educational Inequality*, London: Falmer Press.

Franklin, B. (1995) *The Handbook of Children's Rights: Comparative Policy and Practice*, London: Routledge.

Fuller, M. (1982) 'Young, female and black', in E. Cashmore and B. Troyna (eds) *Black Youth in Crisis*, London: Allen & Unwin.

Furlong, M. (1990) 'Inequality, gender, race and class', Unit 27, Course E205, *Conflictual Change in Education*, Milton Keynes: Open University Press.

Furlong, V.J. (1985) *The Deviant Pupil: Sociological Perspectives*, Milton Keynes: Open University Press.

Galloway, D., Ball, T., Blomfield, D. and Seyd, R. (1982) *Schools and Disruptive Pupils*, London: Longman.

Garner, P. (1994) 'Exclusions from school: towards a new agenda', *Pastoral Care in Education*, 12(4): 3–9.

Gersch, I. and Nolan, A. (1994) 'Exclusions: What the children think', *Educational Psychology in Practice*, 10(1): 35–45.

References

Gewirz, D. (1991) 'Analyses of racism and sexism in education and strategies for change', *British Journal of Sociology of Education*, 12(2): 183–201.

Gillborn, D. (1990) *'Race', Ethnicity and Education: Teaching and Learning in Multi-ethnic Schools*, London: Unwin Hyman.

Gillborn, D. (1997) 'Racism and reform: new ethnicities/old inequalities', *British Educational Research Journal*, 23(3).

Gillborn, D. and Gipps, C. (1996) *Recent Research on the Achievement of Ethnic Minority Pupils*, London: HMSO.

Giroux, H. (1983) *Theory and Resistance in Education: A Pedagogy for the Opposition*, London: Heineman.

Graham, J. and Bowling, B. (1995) *Young People and Crime*, Home Office Research Study 145, London: HMSO.

Hall, S. (1992) 'New ethnicities', in J. Donald and J. Rattansi (eds) *'Race', Culture and Difference*, London: Sage.

Hammersley, M. and Gomm, R. (1993) 'A response to Gillborn and Drew on "race", class and school effects', *New Community*, 19(2): 348–53.

Harrell, P. (1995) 'Do teachers discriminate? Reactions to pupil behaviour' in *Sociology*, 29(1): 58–73.

Hayden, C. (1995) 'Children excluded from primary school: an effect of quasi markets in education?', Conference Paper presented at Youth 2000 International Conference, University of Teesside.

Hayden, C. (1997) *Children Excluded from Primary School*, Milton Keynes: Open University Press.

Hibbert, A. and Fogelman, K. (1988) *Early Adult Outcomes of Truancy*, quoted in E. Blyth and J. Milner (1993).

hooks, b. (1991) *Yearning: Race, Gender and Cultural Politics*, London: Turnaround.

Horvat, E. (1997) 'Structure, standpoint and practices: the construction and meaning of the boundaries of blackness for African-Caribbean female high school services in the college choice process', paper presented at the Annual Conference of the American Educational Research Association, March 1997.

Imich, A.J. (1994) 'Exclusions from school: current trends and issues', *Educational Research*, 36(1): 3–11.

Jeffs, T. (1995) 'Children's educational rights in a new ERA?' in B. Franklin (ed.) *The Handbook of Children's Rights: Comparative Policy and Practice*, London: Routledge.

Keys, W. and Fernandes, C. (1993) 'What do students think about school?', A report for the National Commission on Education, Slough: National Foundation for Educational Research.

Kinder, K., Harland, J., Wilkin, A. and Wakefield, A. (1996a) 'Three to remember: strategies for disaffected pupils', *National Foundation for Educational Research*.

Kinder, K., Wakefield, A. and Wilkin, A. (1996b) 'Talking back: pupil views on disaffection', *National Foundation for Educational Research*.

Kinder, K. and Wilkin, A. (1998) 'With all respect: reviewing disaffection strategies', *National Foundation for Educational Research*.

Lawrence, J., Steed, D. and Young, P. (1984) *Disruptive School*, Orpington: Croom Helm.

Lewisham Education (1993) *Education Statistics Bulletin 1991–1992*, London:

Lewisham Education Authority.

Lloyd-Smith, N. (1993) 'Problem behaviour, exclusions and the policy vacuum', *Pastoral Care in Education*, 11(4): 19–24.

Mac an Ghaill, M. (1988) *Young, Gifted and Black*, Milton Keynes: Open University Press.

Mac an Ghaill, M. (1994) *The Making of Men: Masculinities, Sexualities and Schooling*, Milton Keynes: Open University Press.

Macdonald, I., Bhavnani, R., Khan, L. and John, G. (1989) *Murder in the Playground: The Report of the Macdonald Inquiry into Racism and Racial Violence in Manchester Schools*, London: Longsight Press.

Macey, M. (1992) 'The 1988 Education Reform Act: has multicultural education any future?' *British Journal of Sociology of Education*, 13(1).

McFadden, M. (1995) 'Resistance to schooling and educational outcomes: questions of structure and agency', *British Journal of Sociology of Education*, 16(3): 293–308.

McManus, A. (1987) 'Suspension and exclusion from high schools: the association with catchment and school variables', *School Organization*, 7(3): 261–71.

McManus, M. (1989) *Troublesome Behaviour in the Classroom: A Teacher's Survival Guide*, London: Routledge.

MacPherson Report (Home Office) (1999) 'The Report of the Stephen Lawrence Inquiry chaired by Lord MacPherson', London: HMSO.

McRobbie, A. (1978) 'Working class girls and the culture of femininity' in Women's Study Group (eds) *Women Take Issue: Aspects of Women's Subordination*.

McRobbie, A. (1991) *Feminism and Youth Culture from 'Jackie' to 'Just Seventeen'*, London: Macmillan.

McVicar, M. (1990) 'Education policy: education as a business?', in S. Savage and L. Robbins (eds) *Public Policy Under Thatcher*, London: Macmillan.

Majors, R., Gillborn, D. and Sewell, T. (1998) 'The exclusion of Black children: implications for a racialised perspective', *Multicultural Teaching*, 16(3): 35–7.

Mama, A. (1995) *Beyond the Masks: Race, Gender and Subjectivity 8*, London: Routledge.

Mayet, G. (1992) 'What hope for children with learning and behavioural difficulties?', *Concern*, 82:3.

Mehra, H. (1998) 'The permanent exclusion of Asian pupils in secondary schools in central Birmingham', *Multi-cultural Teaching*, 17(1): 42–8.

Mercer, K. and Julien, I. (1988) 'Race, sexual politics and the black masculinity: a dossier', in R. Champman and J. Rutherford (eds) *Male Order: Unwrapping Masculinities*, London: Lawrence & Wishart.

Metcalf, A. and Humphries, M. (1985) *The Sexuality of Men*, London: Pluto Press.

Meyenn, R. (1980) 'Schoolgirls' peer groups' in P. Woods (ed.) *Pupil Strategies: Explorations in the Sociology of the School*, London: Croom Helm.

Mirza, H. (1992) *Young, Female and Black I*, London: Routledge.

Morgan, G. (1997) *Images of Organization*, California: Sage Publications.

Mortimore, P., Sammons, P., Stoll, L., Lewis, D. and Echo, K. (1988) *School Matters: The Junior Years*, Wells: Open Books.

Nehaul, K. (1996) *The Schooling of Children of Caribbean Heritage*, Stoke-on-Trent: Trentham Books.

Newell, P. (1991) 'The UN Convention and children's rights in the UK', London: National Children's Bureau.

References

Nottingham County Council Education Department (NCCED) (1989) 'Pupil exclusions from Nottingham secondary schools', Advisory and Inspection Service Report No. 15189, Nottingham: County Council Education Department.

Nottingham Ethnic Minorities Consultative Group (1994) Nottingham County Council.

NUT (1992) *Survey on Pupil Exclusions*, London: National Union of Teachers.

OFSTED (Office for Standards in Education) (1993) *Education for Disaffected Pupils 1990–1992*, London: Department of Education.

OFSTED (Office for Standards in Education) (1996) *Exclusions from Secondary Schools 1995–1996*, London: HMSO.

OFSTED (Office for Standards in Education) (1999) *Raising the Attainment of Minority Ethnic Pupils: School and LEA Responses*, London: OFSTED Publications Centre.

Ohrn, E. (1993) 'Gender, influence and resistance in school', *British Journal of Sociology of Education*, 14: 147–58.

Osler, A. (1994) 'The UN Convention on the Rights of the Child: some implications for teacher education', *Educational Review*, 46(2).

Osler, A. (1997) *Exclusion from School and Racial Equality*, London: Commission for Racial Equality.

Parsons, C. (1996) 'Permanent exclusions from schools in the 1990s: Trends, causes and responses', *Children and Society,* 10(3): 255–68.

Parsons, C. et al. (1997) *Exclusions from School: The Public Cost*, London: Commission for Racial Equality.

Pearce, N. and Hillman, J. (1998) *Wasted Youth: Raising Achievement and Tackling Social Exclusion*, London: Institute for Public Policy Research.

Peters, T. and Waterman, R. (1982) *In Search of Excellence: Lessons from America's Best-run Companies*, New York: Harper and Row.

Phoenix, A. (1988) 'Narrow definitions of culture: the case of early motherhood', in S. Westwood and P. Bhachi (eds) *Enterprising Women*, London: Routledge.

Pollitt, C. (1993) *Managerialism and the Public Services: Cuts or Cultural Change in the 1990s*, Oxford: Basil Blackwell.

Prestage, M. (1993) 'Police fear growing tide of exclusions', *Times Educational Supplement*, 19 November.

Pyke, N. (1993) 'Going shopping for truants', *Times Educational Supplement*, 19 November.

Rattansi, A. (1992) 'Changing the subject? Racism, culture and education', in A. Rattansi and J. Donald, *'Race'*, Culture and Differences, Milton Keynes: Open University Press.

Reid, J. (1987) 'A problem in the family: explanations under strain', in T. Booth and D. Coulby (eds) *Producing and Reducing Disaffection*, Milton Keynes: Open University Press.

Reynolds, D. and Cuttance, P. (eds) (1992) *School Effectiveness: Research, Policy and Practice*, London: Cassell.

Reynolds, D., Jones, D. and St Ledger, S. (1976) 'Schools do make a difference', *New Society*, 37(271): 223–5.

Richards, L. and Richards, T. (1994a) 'From filing cabinet to computer', in A. Bryman and R. Burgess (eds) *Analyzing Qualitative Data*, London: Routledge.

Richards, T. and Richards, L. (1994b) 'Using computers in qualitative research' in N. Denzin and Y. Lincoln (eds) *Handbook of Qualitative Research*, California: Sage.

Richardson, R. (1998) 'Inclusive societies, inclusive schools, the terms of debate and action', *Multicultural Teaching*, 16(2): 23–9.

Riddell, S. (1989) 'Pupils, resistance and gender codes: a study of classroom encounters', *Gender and Education*, 1(2), 183–97.

Riley, K. (1985) 'Black girls speak for themselves', in G. Wiener (ed.) *Just a Bunch of Girls*, Milton Keynes: Open University Press, pp. 63–76.

Robinson, K. (1992) 'Classroom discipline: power, resistance and gender – a look at teacher perspectives', *Gender and Education*, 4: 273–87.

Robotham, D. (1995) 'Searching for the truth', *Education*, 186(10): 17–18.

Runnymede Trust (1995) *Challenge, Change and Opportunity, Overview, Text an Agenda*, London: Runnymede Trust.

Runnymede Trust (1996) *This is Where I Live – Stories and Pressures in Brixton*, London: The Runnymede Trust.

Runnymede Trust (1997) *Black Minority and Ethnic Minority Young People and Educational Disadvantage*, London: The Runnymede Trust.

Runnymede Trust (1998) *Improving Practice: A Whole School Approach to Raising the Achievement of African-Caribbean Youth*, London: The Runnymede Trust.

Rutter, M., Maughan, B., Mortimore, P. and Ouston, J. (1979) *Fifteen Thousand Hours*, London: Open Books.

Sasson, D. (1993) 'The price of banishment', *Education* 181(6): 111.

Schein, E.H. (1992) 'What is culture?', in J. Frost et al. (eds), *Reframing Organizational Culture*, California: Sage.

School Standards and Framework Act 1998, London: HMSO.

Sewell, T. (1997) *Black Masculinities and Schooling: How Black Boys Survive Modern Schooling*, Stoke-on-Trent: Trentham Books.

SHA (Secondary Heads Association) (1992) *Excluded from School: A Survey of Suspensions From Secondary Schools in 1991–92*, Leicester: Secondary Heads Association.

Social Exclusion Unit (1998), *Truancy and Social Exclusions*, London: HMSO.

Solomos, J. and Black, L. (1996) *Racism and Society*, Basingstoke: Macmillan.

Stirling, M. (1992) 'The exclusion zone', *Managing Schools*, 1(3): 8–12.

Sultana, R. (1989) 'Transition education, student contestation and the production of meaning: possibilities and limitations of resistance theories', *British Journal of Sociology of Education*, 10(3): 287–309.

Tattum, D.P. (1982) *Disruptive Pupils in School and Units* (Chapter 2), Chichester: John Wiley.

Taylor, M.H. (1992) *Multicultural, Anti-racist Education after ERA*, Slough: National Federation for Educational Research.

TES (*Times Education Supplement*) (1998a) 'Black Exclusions Scandal', p. 13, 18 December.

TES (*Times Education Supplement*) (1998b) 'Blacks 15 times more likely to be excluded', p. 1, 11 December.

Thompson, N. (1997) *Anti-discriminatory Practice*, Basingstoke: Macmillan.

Tizzard, B., Blatchford, P., Burke, J., Farquhar, C. and Plewis, I. (1988) *Young Children at School in Inner City*, London: Routledge.

Troyna, B. (1990) 'Reform or deform? The 1988 Education Reform Act and racial equality in Britain', *New Community*, 16(3).

Vincent, C. (1995) 'School community and ethnic minority parents' in S. Tomlinson and M. Craft (eds) *Ethnic Relations and Schooling*, London: Athlone Press.

References

Walker, J. (1986) 'Romanticising resistance, romanticising culture: problems in Willis' theory of cultural production', *British Journal of Sociology of Education*, 7: 59–80.

Wallace, M. (1979) *Black Macho and the Myth of the Superwoman*, London: John Calder.

Watson, I. (1993) 'Education, class and culture: the Birmingham ethnographic tradition and the problem of the new middle class', *British Journal of Sociology of Education*, 14: 179–97.

Weekes, D. (1996) 'Discourses of blackness and the construction of black femininity', paper presented to the British Psychological Society Annual Conference.

Weekes, D. and Wright, C. (1996) 'Justice, rights and excluding black youth', paper presented to the British Educational Research Association Annual Conference, University of Lancaster.

West, C. (1993) *Race Relations*, Boston: Beacon Press.

Westwood, S. and Bhachi, P. (eds) (1988) *Enterprising Women*, London: Routledge.

Whitney, B. (1993) *The Children Act and Schools*, London: Kogan Page.

Willis, P. (1977) *Learning to Labour: How Working Class Kids Get Working Class Jobs*, Aldershot: Saxon House.

Woods, P. (1990) *The Happiest Days? How Pupils Cope with School*, Lewes: Falmer.

Woods, P. and Hammersley, M. (1993) *Gender and Ethnicity in Schools: Ethnographic Accounts*, London: Routledge.

Wright, C. (1985) 'School processes – an ethnographic study', in J. Eggleston et al. (eds) *Education for Some: The Educational and Vocational Experiences of 15– 18-Year-Old Members of Minority Ethnic Groups*, Stoke-on-Trent: Trentham Books.

Wright, C. (1987) 'The relations between teachers and Afro-Caribbean pupils: observing multi-racial classrooms', in G. Weinger and M. Arnot, *Gender Under Scrutiny: New Inquiries in Education*, London: Hutchinson.

Wright, C. (1992) *Race Relations in the Primary School,* London: David Fulton.

Wright, C., Weekes, D., McGlaughlin, A. and Webb, D. (1998) 'Masculinised discourses within education and the construction of black male identities amongst African-Caribbean youth', *British Journal of Sociology of Education*, 19(1).

Yekwai, D. (1988) *British Racism, Miseducation and the Afrikan Child*, London: Karnak House.

Young, M. and Halsey, A.H. (1995) *Family and Community Socialism*, IPPR Monograph, London: Institute for PUblic Policy Research.

Index

Index